The architect´s
HANDBOOK

CW00976757

LINKS

THE ARCHITECT'S HANDBOOK
Edition 2008

Author: Dimitris Kottas
Conception: Carles Broto
Texts, graphics and design by the author

© Carles Broto i Comerma
Jonqueres, 10, 1-5
08003 Barcelona, Spain
Tel.: +34 93 301 21 99
Fax: +34 93 301 00 21
E-mail: info@linksbooks.net
www.linksbooks.net

ISBN: 978-84-96424-26-5

Index

Geometry
and architectural drawing

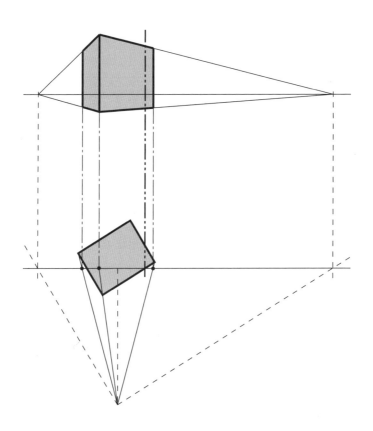

Surfaces and volumes of geometrical bodies

Círcle
Circumference: *pi* x diameter
Surface: *pi* x radius^2
Sector surface: (*pi* x angle x radius^2) : 360

Elypse
Circumference: pi x (1/2 minor axis + 1/2 major axis)
Surface: minor axis x major axis x 0,7854

Parallelogram
Surface: base x height

Triangle
Surface: 1/2 base x height

Pyramid
Surface: (1/2 sum of sides of base x height) +
surface of base
Volume: surface of base x 1/3 height

Sphere
Surface: *pi* x diameter^2
Volume: diameter^3 x 0,5236

Cone
Surface: (*pi* x radius x height) + (ð x radius^2)
Volume: *pi* x radius^2 x 1/2 height

Cylinder
Surface: (*pi* x diameter x height) + (2 x *pi* x radius^2)
Volume: *pi* x radius^2 x height

The Golden Section

The *golden section* or *golden mean* is defined as the ratio between two parts of a line or two dimensions of a plane figure, for the proportion between the smaller part and the larger to be equal to the proportion between the larger part and the whole line.

AB : BC = BC : AC

A   B   C

This proportion is approximately 1:1.6 or 5:8 and it is equal to the proportion between a side and a diagonal of a pentagon.

Construction of a golden rectangle:

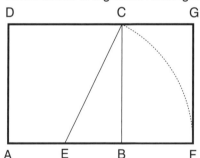

Draw a square ABCD. From point E at the middle of the base AB, draw a line to point C. Draw an arc with radius CE from point C to the base of the square, at point F. The golden rectangle will be ADGF.

The Fibonacci spiral:

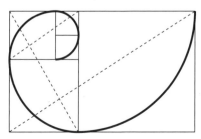

Based on the Fibonacci series, in which each number is the sum of the two preceding numbers, the Fibonacci spiral is constructed inside a series of rectangles which approximate a golden rectangle.

The procedure of a perspective drawing

1. Draw the floor plan in scale at the angle from which it is to be seen.

2. Define the observation point. It is preferable to place it so that the floor plan is contained within a 30^0 angle visual cone.

3. Draw a horizontal line through the floor plan. This is known as the picture plane. The further this line is from the observation point, the larger the drawing will be.

4. Draw two lines parallel to the main sides of the building, going from the observation point to the picture plane. The points at which these lines meet the picture plane are the vanishing points (PF).

5. Draw the horizon line where the perspective drawing is to be. Draw two perpendicular lines from the vanishing points so as to establish the vanishing points on the horizon line.

6. Draw lines from the observation point to the three corners of the floor plan of the building.

7. From the points at which these lines cross the picture plane A, B and C, draw perpendicular lines to the horizon line.

8. Draw a perpendicular line from one of the points at which the floor plan of the building crosses the picture plane. This will be the vertical scale line, on which measurements can be taken using the same scale as that applying to the floor plan. It is preferable for the lowest line of the building to be placed approximately 5 ft 5 inch *(1.65 m)* below the horizon for the drawing to be at a normal height for the human eye.

9. Connect the heights defined on the vertical scale line with the corresponding vanishing points to obtain the building's outline.

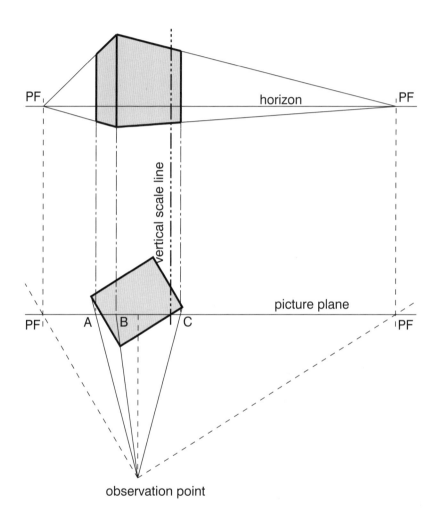

PF

PF

horizon

PF

PF

vertical scale line

picture plane

PF

A

B

C

PF

observation point

Typical sequence of plans for an average size building

Landscape L. Architectural A. Structural S.

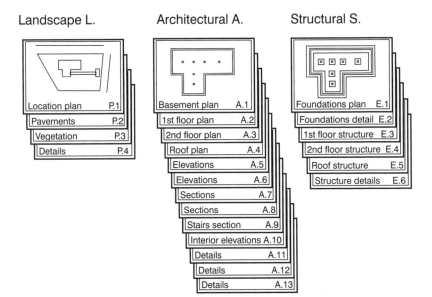

Landscape L.		Architectural A.		Structural S.	
Location plan	P.1	Basement plan	A.1	Foundations plan	E.1
Pavements	P.2	1st floor plan	A.2	Foundations detail	E.2
Vegetation	P.3	2nd floor plan	A.3	1st floor structure	E.3
Details	P.4	Roof plan	A.4	2nd floor structure	E.4
		Elevations	A.5	Roof structure	E.5
		Elevations	A.6	Structure details	E.6
		Sections	A.7		
		Sections	A.8		
		Stairs section	A.9		
		Interior elevations	A.10		
		Details	A.11		
		Details	A.12		
		Details	A.13		

Heating H. Plumbing P. Electricity El.

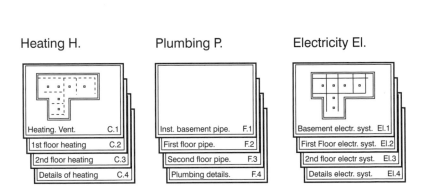

Heating H.		Plumbing P.		Electricity El.	
Heating. Vent.	C.1	Inst. basement pipe.	F.1	Basement electr. syst.	El.1
1st floor heating	C.2	First floor pipe.	F.2	First Floor electr. syst.	El.2
2nd floor heating	C.3	Second floor pipe.	F.3	2nd floor electr syst.	El.3
Details of heating	C.4	Plumbing details.	F.4	Details electr. syst.	El.4

The international DIN system of paper sizes

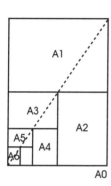
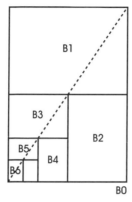
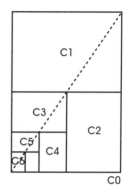

A0   B0   C0

size\class	A series (mm)	B series (mm)	C series (mm)
0	33.110 x 46.810	39.37 x 55.669	36.102 x 51.063
1	23.386 x 33.110	27.835 x 39.37	25.512 x 36.102
2	16.535 x 23.386	19.685 x 27.835	13.031 x 25.512
3	11.693 x 16.535	13.898 x 19.685	12.756 x 13.031
4	8.268 x 11.693	9.843 x 13.898	9.016 x 12.756
5	5.827 x 8.268	6.929 x 9.843	6.378 x 9.016
6	4.134 x 5.827	4.921 x 6.929	4.489 x 6.378
7	2.913 x 4.134	3.465 x 4.921	3.189 x 4.489
8	2.047 x 2.913	2.44 x 3.465	2.244 x 3.189
9	1.457 x 2.047	1.732 x 2.44	
10	1.024 x 1.457	1.22 x 1.732	
11	0.709 x 1.024	0.866 x 1.22	
12	0.512 x 0.709	0.591 x 0.866	

types of paper

class \ size	A series (ft, inch)	B series (ft, inch)	C series (ft, inch)
0	33' 1" x 46' 10"	39' 4" x 55' 8"	36' 1" x 51'
1	23' 5" x 33' 1"	27' 10" x 39' 4"	25' 6" x 36' 1"
2	16' 6" x 23' 5"	19' 8" x 27' 10"	18' x 25' 6"
3	11' 8" x 16' 6"	13' 11" x 19' 8"	12' 9" x 18'
4	8' 3" x 11' 8"	9' 10" x 13' 11"	9' x 12' 9"
5	5' 10" x 8' 3"	6' 11" x 9' 10"	6' 5" x 9'
6	4' 2" x 5' 10"	4' 11" x 6' 11"	4' 6" x 6' 5"
7	2' 11" x 4' 2"	3' 6" x 4' 11"	3' 2" x 4' 6"
8	2' x 2' 11"	2' 5" x 3' 6"	2' 3" x 3' 2"
9	1' 6" x 2'	1' 9" x 2' 5"	
10	1' x 1' 6"	1' 3" x 1' 9"	
11	9" x 1'	10" x 1' 3"	
12	6" x 9"	7" x 10"	

Symbols used in architectural drawings

—————— outlining of main sections

—————— visible edges, outlining of small sections

—————— dimension lines, auxiliary lines

— — — — — hidden edges

■—·—■—·—■ indication of the plane at which a section is made

——-——-——-- axis

····················· elements situated behind the projection plane

masonry of artificial stone

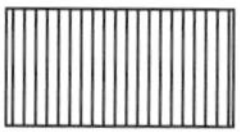

masonry of natural stone

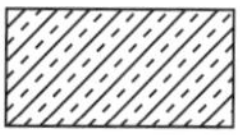

reinforced concrete

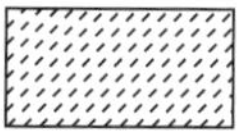

solid concrete

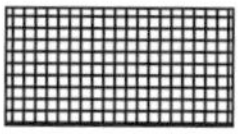

prefabricated concrete elements

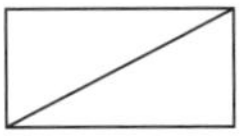

reinforced concrete slab

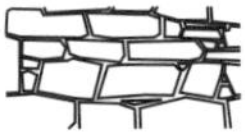

random rubble stonework

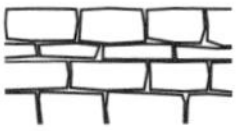

rangework

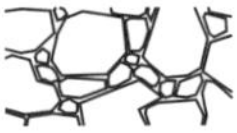

cyclopean stonework

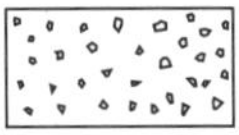

gravel

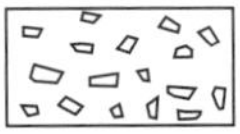

clinker

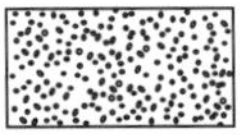

mortar

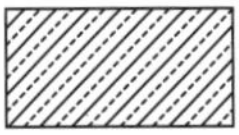

paving slab

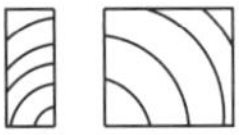

section of wood

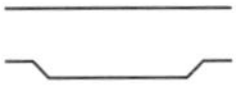

longitudinal steel reinforcement

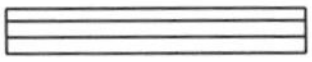

glass

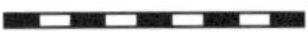

waterproof layer

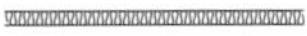

insulation layer

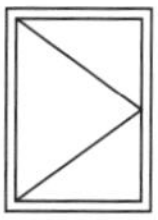

single sash
side hinged

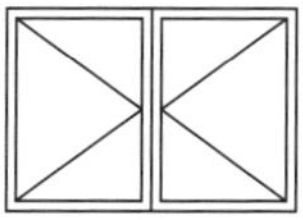

horizontally
sliding sash

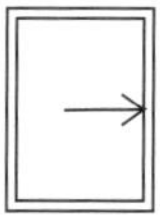

double sash
two side hinged

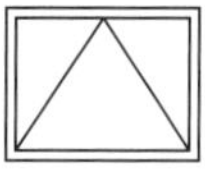

vertically
sliding sash

single sash
bottom hinged

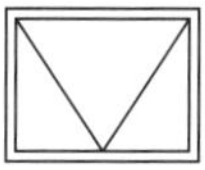

hinged sliding
sash

single sash
top hinged

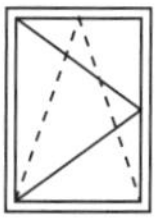

pivoting sliding
sash

side and bottom
hinged

hinged sash
with bolts

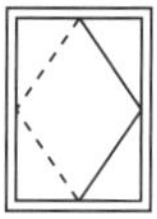

vertical centrally
pivoting sash

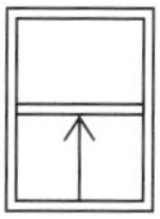

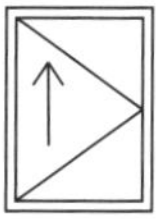

dismountable
sliding sash

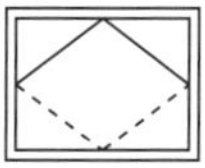

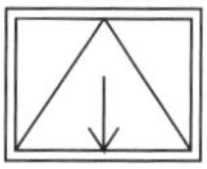

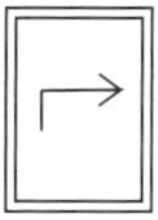

horizontal
centrally pivoting
sash

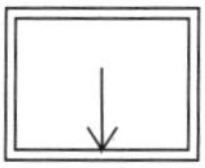

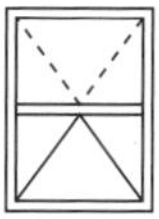

folding door,
accordion door

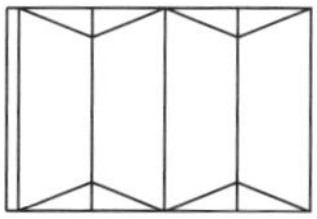

vertically
sliding sash

structural symbols

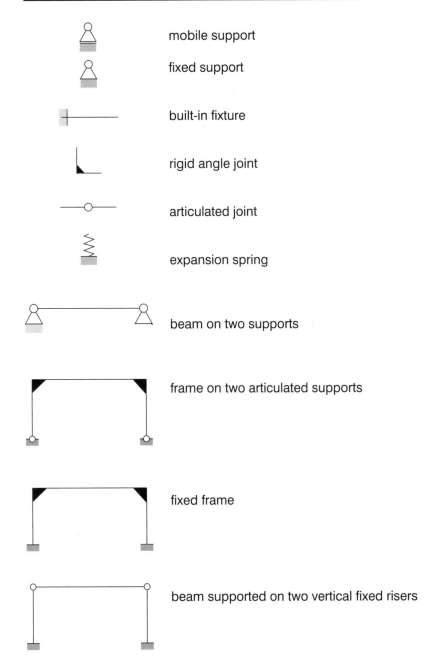

mobile support

fixed support

built-in fixture

rigid angle joint

articulated joint

expansion spring

beam on two supports

frame on two articulated supports

fixed frame

beam supported on two vertical fixed risers

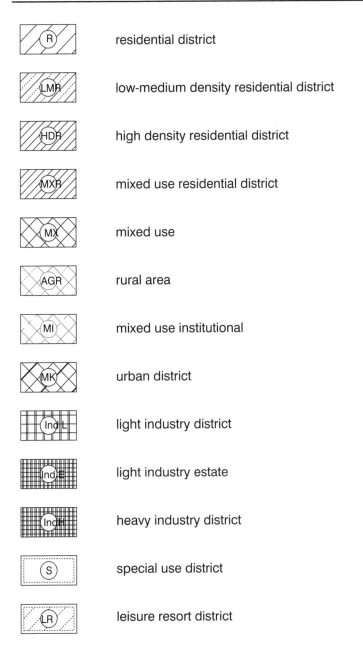

residential district

low-medium density residential district

high density residential district

mixed use residential district

mixed use

rural area

mixed use institutional

urban district

light industry district

light industry estate

heavy industry district

special use district

leisure resort district

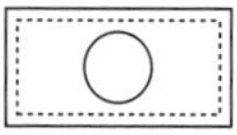

special districts: universities, hospitals, sanatoriums, harbours, commercial centers, etc.

line of construction

limit of construction area

open construction

reserved for single and double family use

reserved for blocks of houses

closed construction

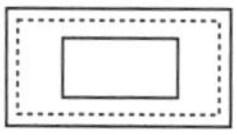

communal space (completed by adding the following signs)

institutional buildings

schools

hospitals

theaters

indoor swimming-pools

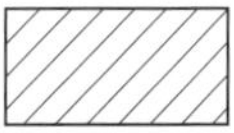

▨	new building	drain of building or yard	⊕
■	existing building	drain of street	
⬚	projected building	closed flow well	
▥	building to be demolished	free flow well	

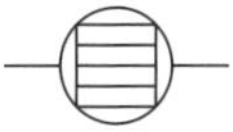

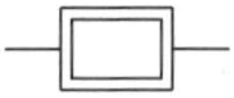

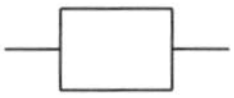

supply network symbols

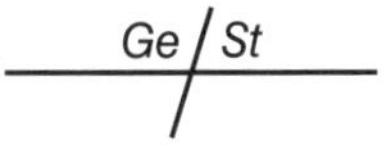

Ge / St

change of conduit material

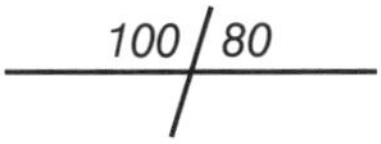

100 / 80

conduit reduction

conduits crossing

conduit switch or valve

branch valve

+

branch line valve

line ending

G

gas meter

W

supply valve

one way valve

800 ⟋ 1000

pressure regulator

———————	water pipe	——/// ——	conductor with labeled wiring
- - - - - - -	built-in water pipe	—— - —— - —	earth wire safety conductor
25 / 20	pipe gauge change	—— - —— - ——	radio and TV wire conductor
—||—	flanged pipe joint		junction box connection
——) ——	male/female pipe joint		earth line
—||—	threaded pipe joint		transformer
W	meter	———————	continuous current
	filter, silt collector		alternate current
	flow control valve	3	three phase current
	gate valve		up-going conductor
	float valve		bottom-to-top conductor
	alternator valve		down-going conductor
	spigot		top-to-bottom conductor

⊏▭⊐	fuse	—— 25 ——	visible pipe
⌀⟋	single wire switch	– – 25 – – –	built-in pipe
⌀⫘	three wire switch	25 ⤬ 20	gauge change
⋀⌀⋀	serial switch	—⊢⊢—	supply closing device
⌀	commuter switch	⟋	up-going pipe
⬤	push button	⟋	permanently up-going pipe
⊗	luminous push button	⟋	down-going pipe
⊗	indicator or pilot light	—┼—	pipes crossing without connecting junction
⟂	single socket	—◆—	cross junction
⟑	double socket	—◆	T junction
●—	empty socket	—⊦⊢—	flange junction
⊓	antenna socket	⊳◁	pressure regulator
✕	lights	⊠ ⊗	chimney or vent shaft

Dimensions of the body and its space in the home

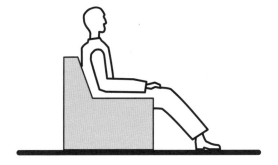

The bodies' dimensions

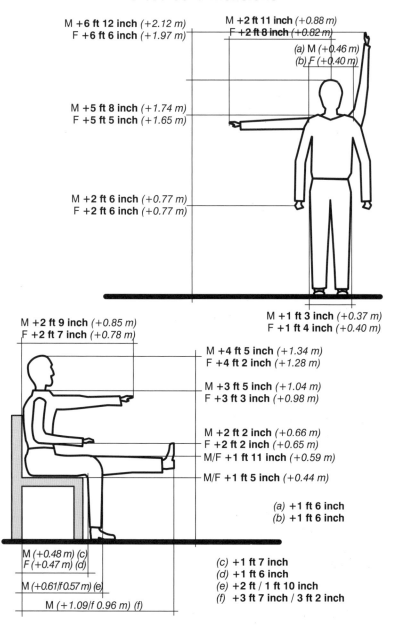

M +6 ft 12 inch *(+2.12 m)*
F +6 ft 6 inch *(+1.97 m)*

M +2 ft 11 inch *(+0.88 m)*
F +2 ft 8 inch *(+0.82 m)*

(a) M *(+0.46 m)*
(b) F *(+0.40 m)*

M +5 ft 8 inch *(+1.74 m)*
F +5 ft 5 inch *(+1.65 m)*

M +2 ft 6 inch *(+0.77 m)*
F +2 ft 6 inch *(+0.77 m)*

M +1 ft 3 inch *(+0.37 m)*
F +1 ft 4 inch *(+0.40 m)*

M +2 ft 9 inch *(+0.85 m)*
F +2 ft 7 inch *(+0.78 m)*

M +4 ft 5 inch *(+1.34 m)*
F +4 ft 2 inch *(+1.28 m)*

M +3 ft 5 inch *(+1.04 m)*
F +3 ft 3 inch *(+0.98 m)*

M +2 ft 2 inch *(+0.66 m)*
F +2 ft 2 inch *(+0.65 m)*
M/F +1 ft 11 inch *(+0.59 m)*

M/F +1 ft 5 inch *(+0.44 m)*

(a) +1 ft 6 inch
(b) +1 ft 6 inch

M *(+0.48 m) (c)*
F *(+0.47 m) (d)*

M *(+0.61/f 0.57 m) (e)*

M *(+1.09/f 0.96 m) (f)*

(c) +1 ft 7 inch
(d) +1 ft 6 inch
(e) +2 ft / 1 ft 10 inch
(f) +3 ft 7 inch / 3 ft 2 inch

living room furniture

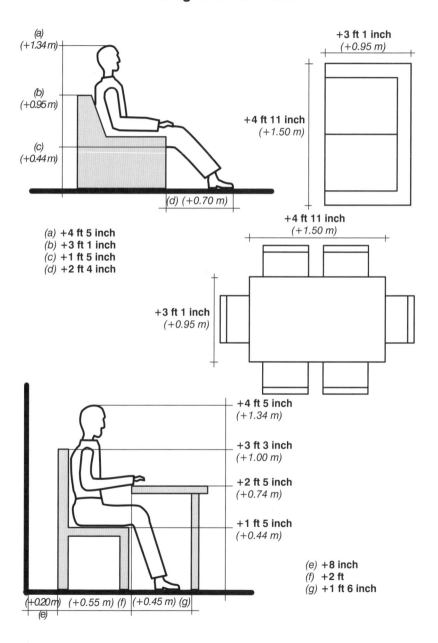

(a) (+1.34 m)

(b) (+0.95 m)

(c) (+0.44 m)

(d) (+0.70 m)

(a) **+4 ft 5 inch**
(b) **+3 ft 1 inch**
(c) **+1 ft 5 inch**
(d) **+2 ft 4 inch**

+3 ft 1 inch
(+0.95 m)

+4 ft 11 inch
(+1.50 m)

+4 ft 11 inch
(+1.50 m)

+3 ft 1 inch
(+0.95 m)

+4 ft 5 inch
(+1.34 m)

+3 ft 3 inch
(+1.00 m)

+2 ft 5 inch
(+0.74 m)

+1 ft 5 inch
(+0.44 m)

(+0.20 m) (+0.55 m) (f) (+0.45 m) (g)
(e)

(e) **+8 inch**
(f) **+2 ft**
(g) **+1 ft 6 inch**

25

Kitchen furniture

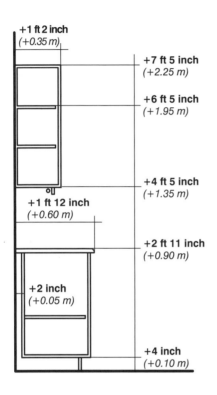

+1 ft 2 inch
(+0.35 m)

+7 ft 5 inch
(+2.25 m)

+6 ft 5 inch
(+1.95 m)

+4 ft 5 inch
(+1.35 m)

+1 ft 12 inch
(+0.60 m)

+2 ft 11 inch
(+0.90 m)

+2 inch
(+0.05 m)

+4 inch
(+0.10 m)

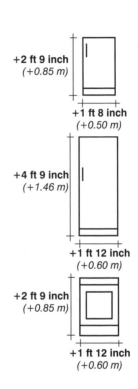

+2 ft 9 inch
(+0.85 m)

+1 ft 8 inch
(+0.50 m)

+4 ft 9 inch
(+1.46 m)

+1 ft 12 inch
(+0.60 m)

+2 ft 9 inch
(+0.85 m)

+1 ft 12 inch
(+0.60 m)

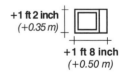

+1 ft 2 inch
(+0.35 m)

+1 ft 8 inch
(+0.50 m)

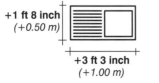

+1 ft 8 inch
(+0.50 m)

+3 ft 3 inch
(+1.00 m)

+3 ft 11 inch
(+1.20 m)

+3 ft 3 inch
(+1.00 m)

Sanitary fixtures

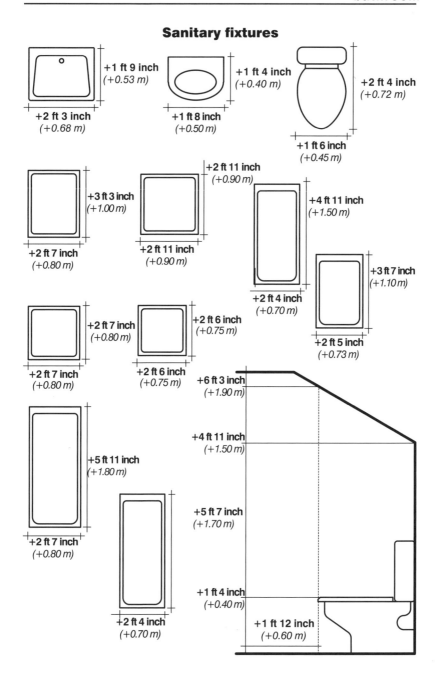

+1 ft 9 inch
(+0.53 m)

+2 ft 3 inch
(+0.68 m)

+1 ft 4 inch
(+0.40 m)

+1 ft 8 inch
(+0.50 m)

+2 ft 4 inch
(+0.72 m)

+1 ft 6 inch
(+0.45 m)

+3 ft 3 inch
(+1.00 m)

+2 ft 7 inch
(+0.80 m)

+2 ft 11 inch
(+0.90 m)

+2 ft 11 inch
(+0.90 m)

+4 ft 11 inch
(+1.50 m)

+2 ft 4 inch
(+0.70 m)

+3 ft 7 inch
(+1.10 m)

+2 ft 5 inch
(+0.73 m)

+2 ft 7 inch
(+0.80 m)

+2 ft 7 inch
(+0.80 m)

+2 ft 6 inch
(+0.75 m)

+2 ft 6 inch
(+0.75 m)

+6 ft 3 inch
(+1.90 m)

+4 ft 11 inch
(+1.50 m)

+5 ft 11 inch
(+1.80 m)

+5 ft 7 inch
(+1.70 m)

+2 ft 7 inch
(+0.80 m)

+1 ft 4 inch
(+0.40 m)

+2 ft 4 inch
(+0.70 m)

+1 ft 12 inch
(+0.60 m)

27

Bedroom furniture

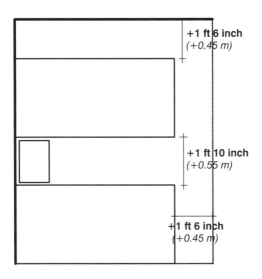

+1 ft 6 inch
(+0.45 m)

+1 ft 10 inch
(+0.55 m)

+1 ft 6 inch
(+0.45 m)

(a) **+2 ft 6 inch** *(+0.75 m)*
(b) **+2 ft 12 inch** *(+0.90 m)*
(c) **+4 ft 5 inch** *(+1.35 m)*
(d) **+4 ft 11 inch** *(+1.50 m)*
(e) **+5 ft 11 inch** *(+1.80 m)*

bed sizes **+6 ft 7 inch**
(+2.00 m)

+6 ft 3 inch
(+1.90 m)

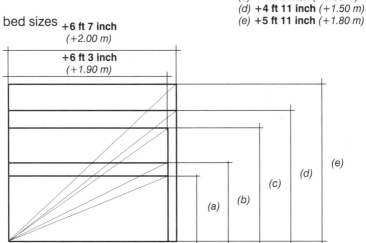

(a) (b) (c) (d) (e)

Design for the handicapped

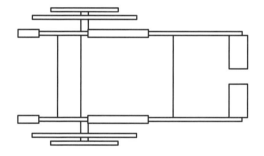

Average dimensions

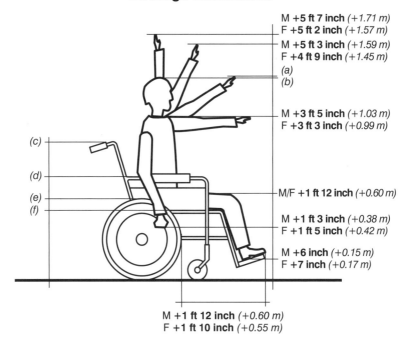

M +5 ft 7 inch *(+1.71 m)*
F +5 ft 2 inch *(+1.57 m)*
M +5 ft 3 inch *(+1.59 m)*
F +4 ft 9 inch *(+1.45 m)*
(a)
(b)

M +3 ft 5 inch *(+1.03 m)*
F +3 ft 3 inch *(+0.99 m)*

M/F +1 ft 12 inch *(+0.60 m)*

M +1 ft 3 inch *(+0.38 m)*
F +1 ft 5 inch *(+0.42 m)*

M +6 inch *(+0.15 m)*
F +7 inch *(+0.17 m)*

(c)
(d)
(e)
(f)

M +1 ft 12 inch *(+0.60 m)*
F +1 ft 10 inch *(+0.55 m)*

(a) M +4 ft 8 inch *(+1.41 m)* / F +4 ft 3 inch *(+1.29 m)*
(b) M +4 ft 4 inch *(+1.33 m)* / F +4 ft 1 inch *(+1.25 m)*
(c) +3 ft 2 inch *(+0.96 m)*
(d) +2 ft 4 inch *(+0.71 m)*
(e) +1 ft 10 inch *(+0.56 m)*
(f) +1 ft 7 inch *(+0.48 m)*

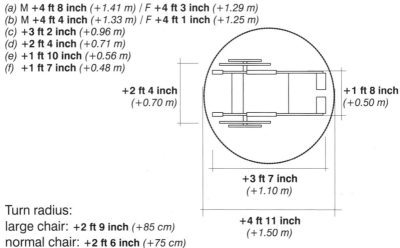

+2 ft 4 inch
(+0.70 m)

+1 ft 8 inch
(+0.50 m)

+3 ft 7 inch
(+1.10 m)

+4 ft 11 inch
(+1.50 m)

Turn radius:
large chair: **+2 ft 9 inch** *(+85 cm)*
normal chair: **+2 ft 6 inch** *(+75 cm)*
small chair (indoor): **+2 ft 4 inch** *(+70 cm)*

spaces

Circulation areas

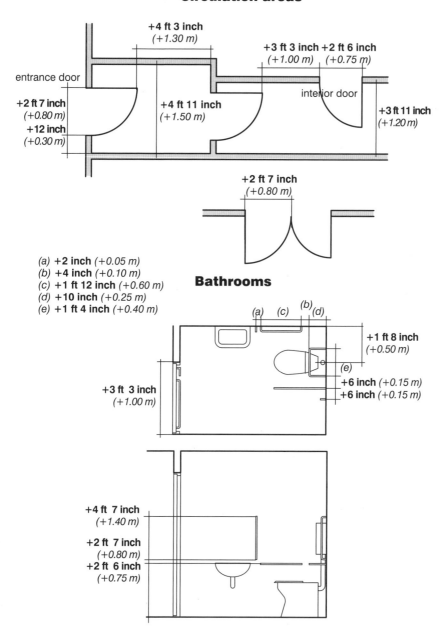

+4 ft 3 inch
(+1.30 m)

+3 ft 3 inch **+2 ft 6 inch**
(+1.00 m) *(+0.75 m)*

entrance door

+2 ft 7 inch
(+0.80 m)
+12 inch
(+0.30 m)

+4 ft 11 inch
(+1.50 m)

interior door

+3 ft 11 inch
(+1.20 m)

+2 ft 7 inch
(+0.80 m)

(a) **+2 inch** *(+0.05 m)*
(b) **+4 inch** *(+0.10 m)*
(c) **+1 ft 12 inch** *(+0.60 m)*
(d) **+10 inch** *(+0.25 m)*
(e) **+1 ft 4 inch** *(+0.40 m)*

Bathrooms

(a) (c) (b) (d)

+1 ft 8 inch
(+0.50 m)

(e)

+6 inch *(+0.15 m)*
+6 inch *(+0.15 m)*

+3 ft 3 inch
(+1.00 m)

+4 ft 7 inch
(+1.40 m)

+2 ft 7 inch
(+0.80 m)
+2 ft 6 inch
(+0.75 m)

Public Buildings

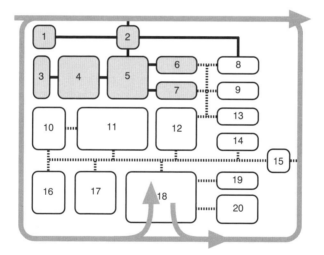

Net floor area per person in different public buildings

Type of space	net floor area (ft²)	n/gr.
Bars	+18 ft² 3 inch² (+1.70 m²)	1.3
Libraries - public space	+34 ft² 12 inch² (+3.25 m²)	1.5
Libraries - storage space(per book)	+9 inch² (+0.07 m²)	1.3
Cafés - tables	+13 ft² 12 inch² (+1.30 m²)	1.5
Cafés - kitchen	+9 ft² 2 inch² (+0.85 m²)	1.5
Clubs	+24 ft² 9 inch² (+2.30 m²)	1.5
Schools - schoolrooms	+15 ft² (+1.40 m²)	1.6
Schools - small schoolrooms	+19 ft² 11 inch² (+1.85 m²)	1.6
Schools -laboratories	+69 ft² 11 inch² (+6.50 m²)	1.6
Gymnasiums	+50 ft² (+4.65 m²)	1.4
Hospitals - beds	+124 ft² 10 inch² (+11.6 m²)	1.6
Hospitals - personnel	+45 ft² 2 inch² (+4.20 m²)	1.3
Hotels - bedrooms	+119 ft² 5 inch² (+11.1 m²)	1.6
Hotels - lobby	+10 ft² 3 inch² (+0.95 m²)	1.4
Museums - exhibition area	+15 ft² (+1.40 m²)	1.2
Museums - vestibule, shop	20% of exhib.	
Museums - personnel	+150 ft² 8 inch² (+14.0 m²)	1.3
Offices - private	+150 ft² 8 inch² (+14.0 m²)	1.3
Offices - semi-private	+119 ft² 5 inch² (+11.1 m²)	1.3
Restaurants - tables	+13 ft² 12 inch² (+1.30 m²)	1.5
Restaurants - kitchen	+6 ft² 12 inch² (+0.65 m²)	1.5
Meeting rooms (minus seating)	+6 ft² 12 inch² (+0.65 m²)	2.5
Meeting rooms (plus seating)	+10 ft² 9 inch² (+1.00 m²)	2.2
Conference rooms	+15 ft² (+1.40 m²)	2.0
Theaters - foyer	+10 ft² 3 inch² (+0.95 m²)	1.2
Shops	+39 ft² 10 inch² (+3.70 m²)	1.3

The n/gr. factor refers to a ratio between net and gross floor area of the building. Gross floor area does not usually include stairs, elevator shafts or spaces with a floor to ceiling distance below 6 feet.

Sanitary areas in public buildings

Separate sanitary areas for men and women are required.
There must be one handbasin for every five urinals.
In most public buildings there must be a minimum of two water closets, in case one of them is out of operation.
At least one sanitary area for the handicapped is required.

Offices and shops

Up to 15 persons	1 hand basin
16 - 30	2
31 - 50	3
51 - 75	4
76 - 100	5
over 100	1 more for every additional 25 persons

FACTORIES
water closets: 1 for every 25 persons
basin: From1 for every 20 persons to 1 for every 5 depending on the type of work involved.

RESTAURANTS

MEN
water closets: 1 for every 100 persons up to 400 personas, plus 1 for every 250 additional persons.
urinals: 1 for every 25 persons
basins: 1 for every water closet and 1 for every 5 urinals
WOMEN
water closets: 2 for every 100 persons up to 200 persons, plus 1 for every 100 additional persons.
basins: 1 for every 2 water closets

THEATERS AND ENTERTAINMENT HALLS

MEN
water closets: 1 up to 250 persons, plus 1 for every 500 additional persons.
urinals: 2 up to 100 persons, plus 1 for every 80 additional persons.
WOMEN
water closets: 2 up to 50 persons, 3 up to 100 persons, plus 1 for every 40 additional persons.
basins: 1 for every 2 water closets

Organization of a large enterprise

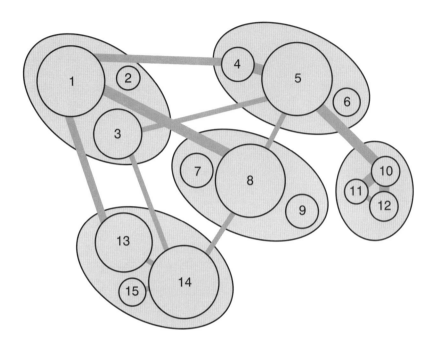

1. Financial planning
2. Internal affairs
3. Financial operations
4. Engineers
5. Product control
6. Purchases
7. New installation plans
8. Production data
9. Factory engineers
10. Invoice control
11. Order completion programs
12. Personnel
13. Electrical and mechanical installations
14. Production
15. Factory

The diagram shows the relative magnitude of several groups and the manner in which they interrelate.

Organization of a Post Office branch

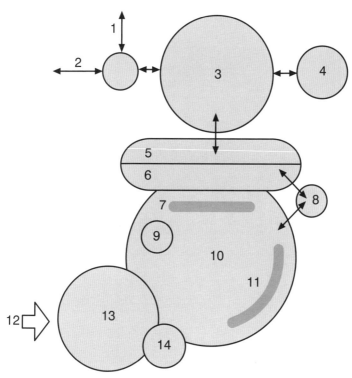

1. Mail distribution
2. Security
3. Administration
4. Financial operations
5. Personnel area
6. Windows
7. Queues
8. Security
9. Open assistance counters
10. Public areas
11. Stamp vendors
12. Entrance
13. Foyer
14. Mail boxes and automatic stamp vending machines

Organization of a banking office branch

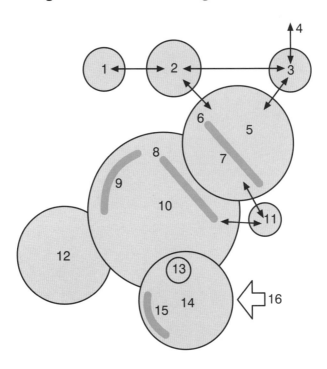

1. High security area
2. Security area
3. Administration - personnel
4. Emergency exit
5. Offices area
6. Windows
7. Cashiers
8. Queues
9. Counters
10. Public area
11. Security control
12. Interviews
13. Reception
14. Foyer open 24 hours
15. Automatic cash dispensers
16. Entrance

Reception furniture

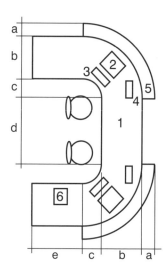

1. Work desk

2. Computer screen

3. Keyboard

4. Printer

5. Counter for the visitors

6. Security screen

7. Vertical non-transparent surface(conceals feet and the electrical wiring of computers)

a. Shelf for visitors: **+10 inch** *(+20-25 cm)*

b. Table: **+1-2 ft 12-6 inch** *(+60-75 cm)*

c. Radio **+0-1 ft 12-4 inch** *(+30-40 cm)*

d. Table width: **+2-3 ft 11-7 inch** *(+90-110 cm)*

e. Table side: **+2-2 ft 4-11 inch** *(+70-90 cm)*

f. Total screen height: **+3-3 ft 3-11 inch** *(+100-120 cm)*

g. Counter height: **+3-3 ft 3-5 inch** *(+100-105 cm)*

h. Table height: **+2-2 ft 4-6 inch** *(+70-75 cm)*

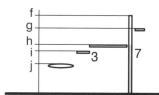

i. Keyboard: **+1-2 ft 11-4 inch** *(+58-70 cm)*

j. Chair: **+0-1 ft 12-8 inch** *(+30-50 cm)*

Diagram of the organization of a school

1. Classroom
2. Changing room
3. Sanitary area
4. Science classroom
5. Common area
6. Dining hall
7. Library
8. Doctor
9. Teacher's offices
10. Head office
11. Reception
12. Hall

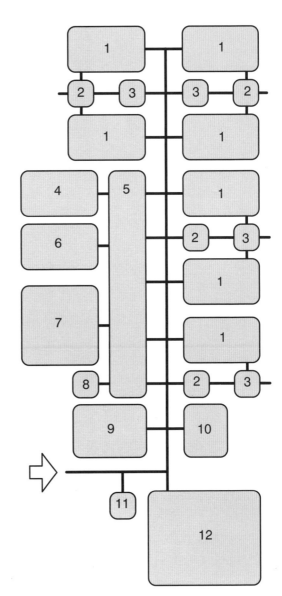

Furniture

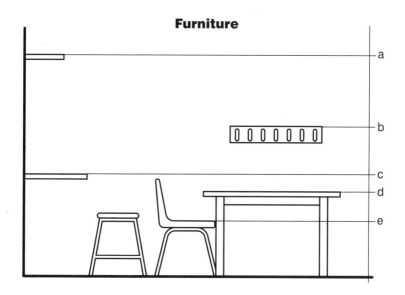

furniture	age					
	3 - 4	5 - 7	8 - 12	11 - 14	14 - 16	16 - 18
a: Shelf	+3 ft 3 inch	+3 ft 11 inch	+4 ft 6 inch	+4 ft 12 inch	+5 ft 6 inch	+5 ft 8 inch
b: Cl. hanger	+2 ft 8 inch	+3 ft	+3 ft 7 inch	+4 ft 2 inch	+4 ft 7 inch	+4 ft 9 inch
c: Bench	+1 ft 10 inch	+2 ft	+2 ft 5 inch	+2 ft 9 inch	+2 ft 9 inch	+2 ft 10 inch
d: Table	+1 ft 6 inch	+1 ft 9 inch	+1 ft 11 inch	+2 ft	+2 ft 4 inch	+2 ft 4 inch
e: Chair	+10 inch	+12 inch	+1 ft 1 inch	+1 ft 3 inch	+1 ft 5 inch	+1 ft 5 inch

furniture	age (mm)					
	3 - 4	5 - 7	8 - 12	11 - 14	14 - 16	16 - 18
a: Shelf	1005	1195	1355	1515	1675	1715
b: Cl. hanger	820	920	1095	1275	1385	1450
c: Bench	555	625	730	825	830	870
d: Table	460	520	580	640	700	700
e: Chair	260	300	340	380	420	420

Organization of a drama, opera or dance theater

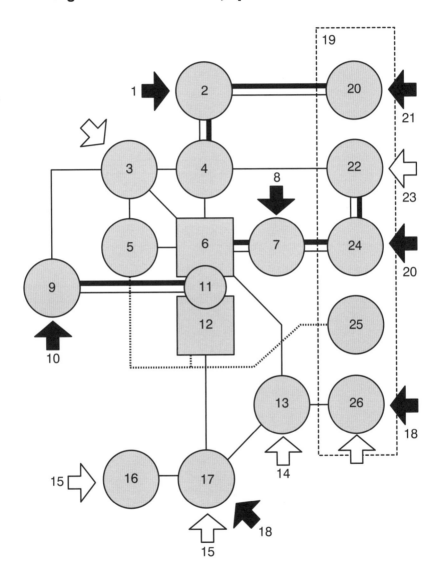

1. Entrance to changing rooms
2. Costumes wardrobe
3. Stage entrance
4. Actors' canteen and dressing rooms
5. Performance organization
6. Stage
7. Scenery storage space
8. Entrance to stage
9. Musicians' room
10. Musical instrument storage
11. Orchestra pit
12. Spectators' seating area
13. Management offices
14. Access to offices
15. Main entrance for public use
16. Ticket windows
17. Foyer
18. Catering supplies entrance
19. Production areas
20. Costumes wardrobe
21. Materials entrance door
22. Rehearsal space
23. Alternative entrance for public use
24. Scenery workshop
25. Recording studio
26. Production offices

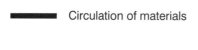 Circulation of materials

Circulation of persons

 Entrance of materials

 Entrance of persons

If the theater is only used for the performances and the production is executed elsewhere there are no production spaces on site but the rest of the diagram remains unchanged. If musical or dance performances are not envisaged the orchestra pit and the musicians' room disappear from the diagram.

Slope in a theater

A: Horizontal distance between the first row and the backstage wall.
B: Horizontal distance between rows. Between 800 and 1150 mm.
C: Vertical distance between the level of the stage and the height of the eyes in the first row. When this distance is zero we know the maximum height of the stage (approx. 1060 mm) The height of the eyes is considered to be 1020-1220 mm from the floor.
D: Vertical distance between rows.
E: Necessary increase in the height of the eyes from one row to the next. Normally 120 mm. It may be up to 60 mm to see the between the heads of the row in front.
n: Number of rows.

$$D = B/A \,[C + (n-1) + E]$$

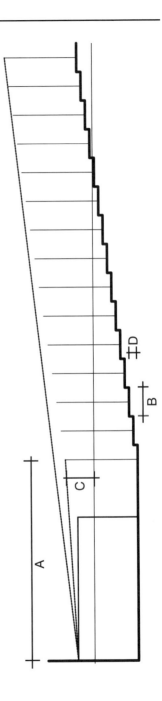

Organization of a public library

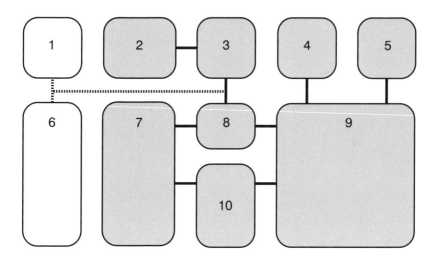

1. Storage
2. Conference hall
3. Entrance
4. Workroom for groups
5. Work and reading spaces
6. Management
7. Children's hall
8. Registry and files
9. Adults' hall
10. Consulting room

⬜ Spaces open to the public
⬜ Spaces for the personnel
— Circulation of the public
⋯⋯ Circulation of the personnel

Organization of a hotel

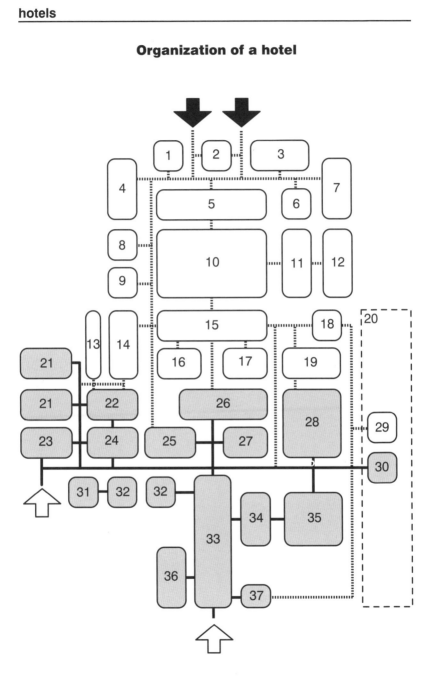

1. Waste disposal
2. Control
3. Laundry
4. Storage
5. Kitchen storage
6. Office
7. Sanitary area, personnel changing rooms
8. Technicians
9. Maintenance
10. Kitchen
11. Kitchen for personnel
12. Canteen for personnel
13. Furniture storage
14. Sanitary service
15. General sanitary service
16. Drinks
17. Washing up
18. Bedroom service
19. Cafeteria kitchen
20. Bedrooms
21. Private bedrooms
22. Dance hall
23. Bar
24. Lobby
25. Bar
26. Restaurant
27. Lounge
28. Café
29. Personnel elevator
30. Guests' elevators
31. Cloak-room
32. Washrooms
33. Central foyer
34. Reception
35. Administration
36. Shops
37. Luggage storage

▢ Areas for the public

◯ Areas for the personnel

— Public circulation

⸱⸱⸱⸱ Personnel circulation

Typical kitchen of a restaurant

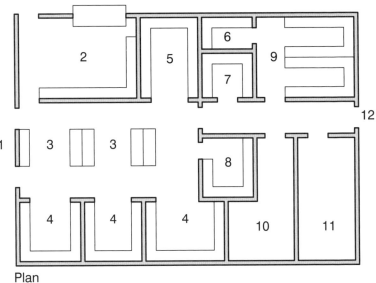

Plan

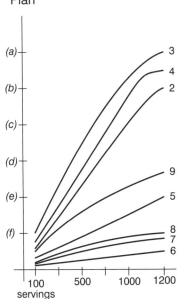

Space needed according to number
of meals served per day.

1. Dining room
2. Washing up dishes/cutlery
3. Production
4. Preparation
5. Washing up pots/pans
6. Cleaning materials
7. Deep-freezer
8. Refrigerator
9. Store non-perishables
10. Personnel sanitation
11. Personnel changing rm.
12. Personnel Entrance

(a) **+645 ft² 7 inch²** *(+60 m²)*
(b) **+538 ft²** *(+50 m²)*
(c) **+430 ft² 5 inch²** *(+40 m²)*
(d) **+322 ft² 10 inch²** *(+30 m²)*
(e) **+215 ft² 2 inch²** *(+20 m²)*
(f) **+107 ft² 7 inch²** *(+10 m²)*

Restaurant furniture

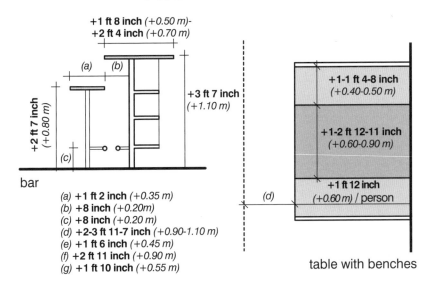

+1 ft 8 inch *(+0.50 m)-*
+2 ft 4 inch *(+0.70 m)*

(a) (b)

+3 ft 7 inch
(+1.10 m)

+2 ft 7 inch
(+0.80 m)

(c)

bar

(a) **+1 ft 2 inch** *(+0.35 m)*
(b) **+8 inch** *(+0.20m)*
(c) **+8 inch** *(+0.20 m)*
(d) **+2-3 ft 11-7 inch** *(+0.90-1.10 m)*
(e) **+1 ft 6 inch** *(+0.45 m)*
(f) **+2 ft 11 inch** *(+0.90 m)*
(g) **+1 ft 10 inch** *(+0.55 m)*

+1-1 ft 4-8 inch
(+0.40-0.50 m)

+1-2 ft 12-11 inch
(+0.60-0.90 m)

(d)

+1 ft 12 inch
(+0.60 m) / person

table with benches

distribution of tables

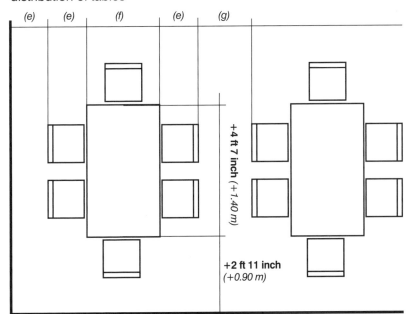

(e)   (e)   (f)   (e)   (g)

+4 ft 7 inch *(+1.40 m)*

+2 ft 11 inch
(+0.90 m)

Organization of a museum

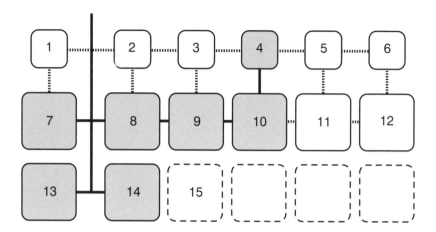

1. Administration, public relations
2. Education
3. Design and production
4. Library
5. Documentation, research and security
6. Purchases
7. Shop
8. Foyer
9. Showrooms
10. Storage
11. Closed storage
12. Restoring
13. Café, restaurant
14. Conference room
15. Posible extensions

Areas for the public
Areas for the personnel
Circulation of the public
Circulation of personnel

Show case illumination

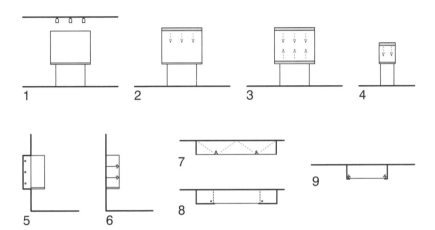

1. Exterior lighting from above. It is better to use "cold" lamps. The objects may cast shadows if they are illuminated with slanted lighting.

2. Interior lighting from above. The light boxes are separated from the show cases with a translucent glass or a grid with a transparent glass. Fluorescent lamps may be used for the homogenous lighting or incandescent lamps to highlight objects.

3. Interior lighting from above and below, so as to avoid shadows and illuminate the lower side of the objects. The light source must be covered.

4. Internal lighting. Luminosity at eye level must be controlled. An electrical lead must be extended to the showcase.

5. Lighting from behind. Fluorescent tubes behind a translucent glass. There must be a distance between the tubes and the glass.

6. Lighting by tubes placed at the corner of the shelves to illuminate each shelf from below and above. This may only be used with low invulnerability objects.

7. Fluorescent lighting. It is placed at the front of the showcase, behind the risers of the frame without translucent glass. Luminosity at eye level must be controlled.

8. Lateral lighting. The tubes must be covered with translucent material.

9. Lighting with vertical tubes. Placed at the corners forming light pillars. It is a good solution for showcases with solid sides.

Showcase opening systems

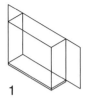

1

2

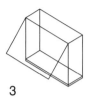

3

4

5

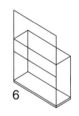

6

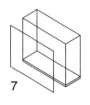

7

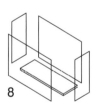

8

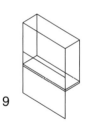

9

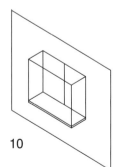

10

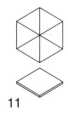

11

1. Sides with hinges. It offers good visibility but the size of the showcase must be limited.

2. Front with hinges. Easier to use. A central riser is required for large showcases.

3. A front with hinges above. Strong secure wall fixtures are necessary.

4. Two sliding panels. Used when space at the sides is limited. A sealer is required where the panels meet, which may impare visibility.

5. Sliding front. Good visibility and good access to the showcase interior. Large sheets of glass need support when they open.

6. Front slides upward. The weight of the glass may cause problems. A strong closing mechanism is required.

7. Dismountable front. Offers good visibility and good access to the interior. If the glass is large two people are needed to dismount it.

8. Dismountable showcase. Used for travelling or temporary exhibitions. A large team is needed for moving assembly.

9. Downward sliding front.

10. Access from behind. Good for long showcases. Space at the back is needed for access to the showcase interior. It is hard to see the display of the objects and alter it from the back once they are installed.

11. Raisable showcase. It offers very good visibility if it is well constructed. Its weight means it is only usable in small sizes, so as not to endanger the integrity of the exhibits.

Organization of a bus station

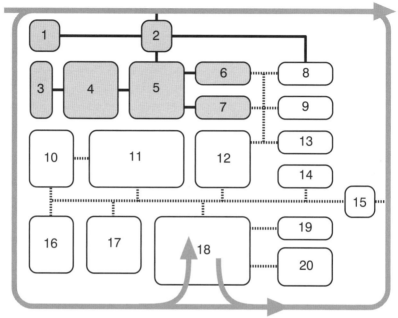

1. Newstand kiosk
2. Loading bay
3. Public washrooms
4. Cafeteria
5. Foyer
6. Left luggage and lost property desks
7. Information, tickets
8. Management
9. Station inspector
10. Staff washrooms and changing rooms
11. Staff cafeteria
12. Office
13. Inspector
14. Head office
15. Staff loading bay
16. Maintenance staff washrooms and changing rooms
17. Dining room
18. Maintenance
19. Storage
20. Maintenance

Football
344 ft 6 inch x 229 ft 8 inch
(105 x 70 m)
goals **24 ft x 8 ft** *(7.32 x 2.44 m)*

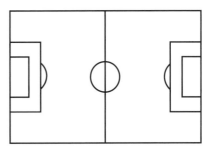

Small footbal fields
144 ft 4 inch x 72 ft 2 inch
(44 x 22 m)
goals **24 ft x 8 ft** *(7.32 x 2.44 m)*

Basketball
85 ft 4 inch x 45 ft 11 inch
(26 x 14 m)
basket: height **10 ft** *(3.05 m)*

Volleyball
59 ft x 29 ft 6 inch
(18 x 9 m)

Handball (indoors)
144 ft 4 inch x 72 ft 2 inch
(44 x 22 m)
goals **9 ft 10 inch x 6 ft 7 inch**
(3.00 x 2.00 m)

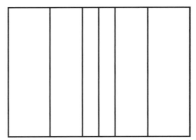

European Rugby football
328 ft 1 inch x 224 ft 5 inch
(100 x 68.4 m)
goals **18 ft 7 inch x 9 ft 10 inch**
(5.67 x 3.00 m)

Tennis
35 ft 12 inch x 77 ft 12 inch
(10.97 x 23.77 m)
Perimetral space **59 ft 11 inch x**
119 ft 12 inch *(18.27 x 36.57 m)*
height of net: **3 ft** *(0.915 m)* (center),
3 ft 6 inch *(1.06 m)* (posts)

Environmentally friendly architecture

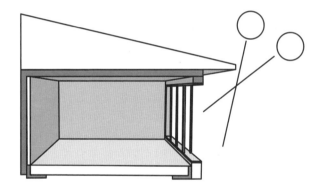

solar angle and heat flow

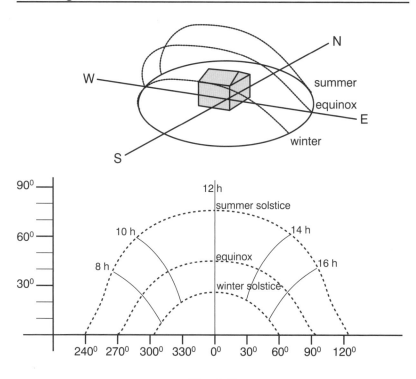

Heat flow

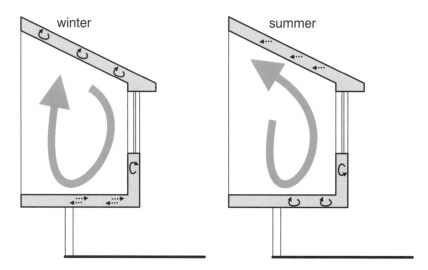

Passive solar heating

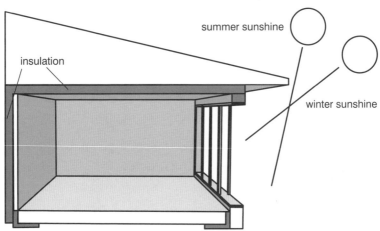

summer sunshine

insulation

winter sunshine

Concrete floor with a dark surface to absorb solar heat

Active solar heating

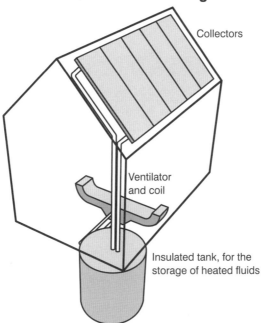

Collectors

Ventilator
and coil

Insulated tank, for the
storage of heated fluids

Mechanisms for the control of solar radiation

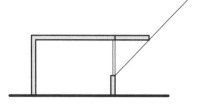

Eaves
A solid opaque overhead projection shelters windows from the sun and rain. Different eaves can be built over each opening.

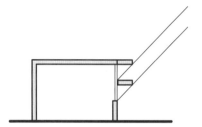

Overhang shelf
A shelf is a horizontal element placed within the window frame. It offers solar protection and can be made of a reflecting material to increase natural illuminance.

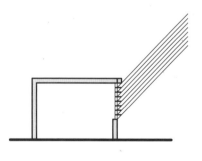

Blinds (horizontal)
A blind consists of horizontal elements that permit air and light to pass while blocking direct solar rays. The elements may be fixed or adjustable, swivelling on horizontal axes to adapt the degree of shelter. There are indoor or outdoor blinds. The outdoor type offers greater thermal shelter but is more exposed to the weather.

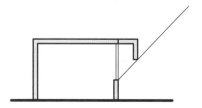

Overhang screen
Said of a vertical element that hangs free of the wall, from a projecting shelf or balcony, increasing the solar barrier provided by an overhang shelf.

Sun screen

A vertical element used to obstruct the solar rays, placed outside the windows, possibly with some separation. It may be solid and opaque or with slats, like a venetian blind.

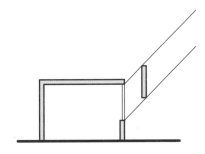

Sun shield roof

A second roof over the normal roof, with a ventilated air space. As well as the windows, it shelters the whole of the roof from the direct effect of solar radiation.

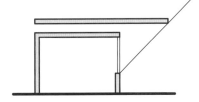

Awning

A fixed or foldable textile covering, that can be adapted to the existing sunlight, as required. It may be translucent, allowing for greater illuminance.

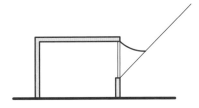

Pergola

A fixed solar protection-screen having a non-solid design of wood or masonry strips permitting sun through intermittently and inviting a growth of climbing vegetation.

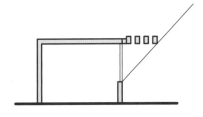

sunlight control

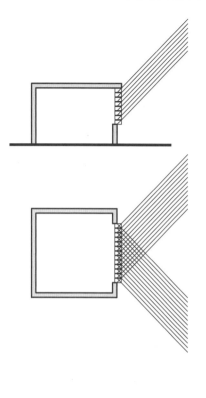

Venetian Blind

A combination of vertical and horizontal slats or some other type of semi-solid gridwork, offering solar protection and some degree of visual shelter.

Double wall

A second wall built a small distance on the outside of the regular wall, to protect the window from the sun, as well as the whole façade.

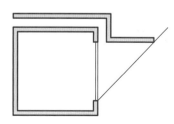

62

Box frame
It combines the advantages of the overhang with those of a lateral shield, forming a deep projecting frame around the windows.

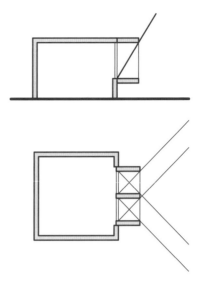

Vegetation
Vegetation is an excellent source of solar protection and radiation control. It allows for seasonal differences in the degree of shelter achieved. Careful choice of the species is required to provide appropriate shelter at all times of the year .

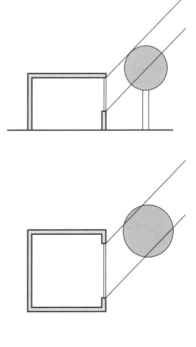

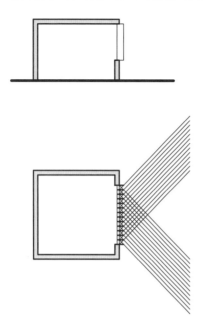

Blinds (vertical)

Vertical blinds operate the same way as horizontal ones and have the same options of being installed indoors or outdoors, possibly swiveling on vertical axes or having only one fixed possition.

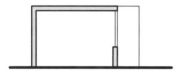

Sun barrier

A vertical element projecting out from the façade to block the solar rays. It may be perpendicular or oblique to the wall surface and may be part of the façade or appear as an independent item.

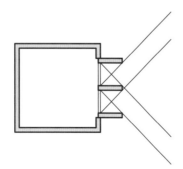

Curtains

Curtains or indoor blinds offer a visual barrier and allow a direct control of the quantity of natural light entering the space. They are not an efficient form of thermal protection because they block solar radiation once it is past the window glass and inside the space.

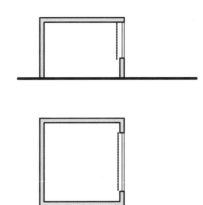

Changing the side the windows open.

When the orientation of a façade is unsuitable, the way the windows open can be altered, to improve solar protection and illuminance levels.

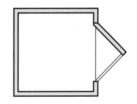

Combinations

Almost all the strategies of sunlight control can be combined so as to achieve the desired result, regarding the double objective of solar protection and the appearance of the building.

Elements of wind protection

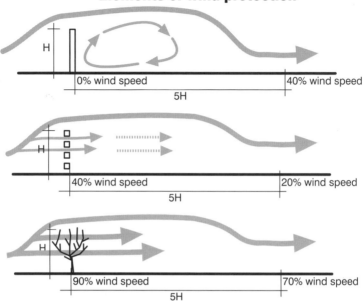

Sheltered space between buildings

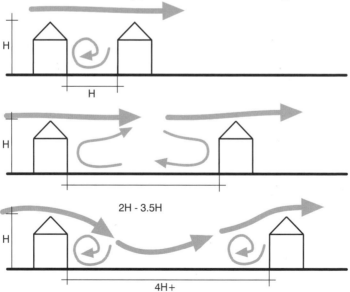

Vehicles

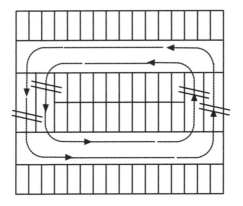

Dimensions of various vehicle types

Vehicle	length (m)	width (m)	height (m)	radius (m)
Bicycle	1.80	0.56	1.10	-
Motorcycle	2.25	0.60	0.80	-
Small car (Mini)	3.05	1.40	1.35	4.80
Regular car	4.00	1.60	1.35	5.25
Large car	4.50	1.70	1.45	5.50
Caravan (mobile home)	4.50	2.10	2.50	-
Truck	7.00	2.50	3.35	8.70
Garbage truck	7.40	2.30	4.00	7.00
Fire engine	8.00	2.50	4.00	7.60

Garage plans for single family homes

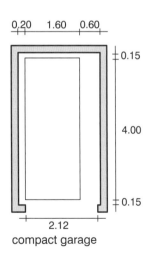

compact garage

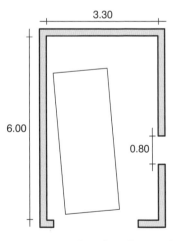

garage for a handicapped person

Dimensions of various vehicle types

Vehicle	length (ft)	width (ft)	height (ft)	radius (ft)
Bicycle	5ft 11inch	1ft 10inch	3ft 7inch	-
Motorcycle	7ft 5inch	1ft 12inch	2ft 7inch	-
Small car (Mini)	10ft	4ft 7inch	4ft 5inch	15ft 9inch
Regular car	13ft 1inch	5ft 3inch	4ft 5inch	17ft 3inch
Large car	14ft 9inch	5ft 7inch	4ft 9inch	18ft
Caravan (mobile home)	14ft 9inch	6ft 11inch	8ft 2inch	-
Truck	22ft 12inch	8ft 2inch	10ft 12inch	28ft 6inch
Garbage truck	24ft 3inch	7ft 7inch	13ft 1inch	22ft 12inch
Fire engine	26ft 3inch	8ft 2inch	13ft 1inch	24ft 11inch

Garage plans for single family homes

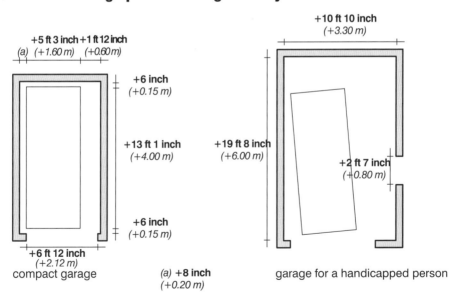

+5 ft 3 inch +1 ft 12 inch
(a) (+1.60 m) (+0.60m)

+6 inch
(+0.15 m)

+13 ft 1 inch
(+4.00 m)

+6 inch
(+0.15 m)

+6 ft 12 inch
(+2.12 m)
compact garage

+10 ft 10 inch
(+3.30 m)

+19 ft 8 inch
(+6.00 m)

+2 ft 7 inch
(+0.80 m)

(a) +8 inch
(+0.20 m)

garage for a handicapped person

Parking space dimensions

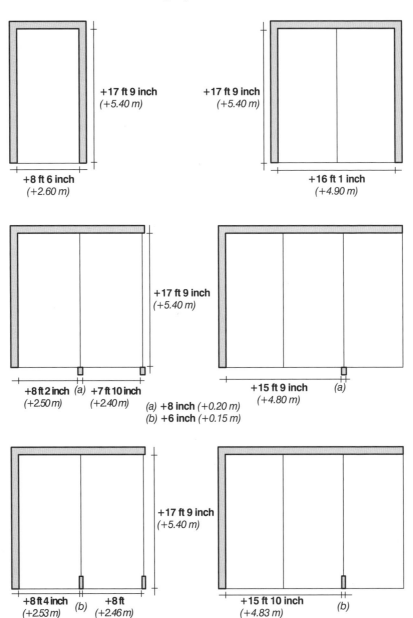

+17 ft 9 inch
(+5.40 m)

+8 ft 6 inch
(+2.60 m)

+17 ft 9 inch
(+5.40 m)

+16 ft 1 inch
(+4.90 m)

+17 ft 9 inch
(+5.40 m)

+8 ft 2 inch *(a)* +7 ft 10 inch
(+2.50 m) (+2.40 m)

(a) +8 inch (+0.20 m)
(b) +6 inch (+0.15 m)

+15 ft 9 inch *(a)*
(+4.80 m)

+17 ft 9 inch
(+5.40 m)

+8 ft 4 inch *(b)* +8 ft
(+2.53 m) (+2.46 m)

+15 ft 10 inch *(b)*
(+4.83 m)

Dimensions of the ramps

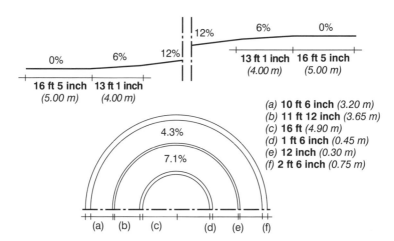

12%

6%   0%

13 ft 1 inch   16 ft 5 inch
(4.00 m)   (5.00 m)

0%   6%   12%

16 ft 5 inch   13 ft 1 inch
(5.00 m)   (4.00 m)

4.3%

7.1%

(a) 10 ft 6 inch (3.20 m)
(b) 11 ft 12 inch (3.65 m)
(c) 16 ft (4.90 m)
(d) 1 ft 6 inch (0.45 m)
(e) 12 inch (0.30 m)
(f) 2 ft 6 inch (0.75 m)

(a)   (b)   (c)   (d)   (e)   (f)

Different floors in a parking space building

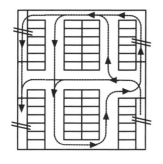

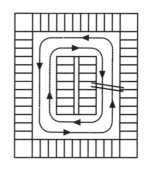

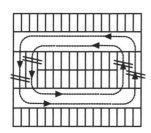

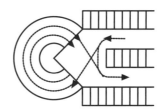

Bicycle parking spaces

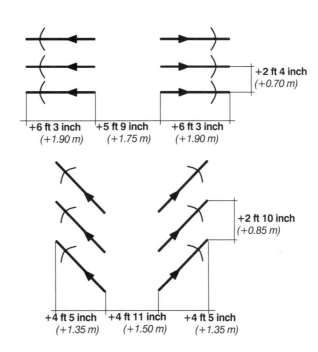

+2 ft 4 inch
(+0.70 m)

+6 ft 3 inch
(+1.90 m)
+5 ft 9 inch
(+1.75 m)
+6 ft 3 inch
(+1.90 m)

+2 ft 10 inch
(+0.85 m)

+4 ft 5 inch
(+1.35 m)
+4 ft 11 inch
(+1.50 m)
+4 ft 5 inch
(+1.35 m)

Bicycle lane

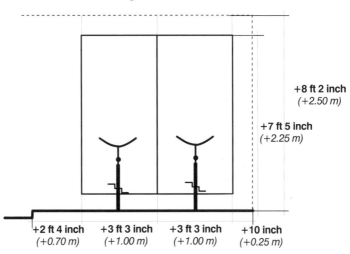

+8 ft 2 inch
(+2.50 m)

+7 ft 5 inch
(+2.25 m)

+2 ft 4 inch
(+0.70 m)
+3 ft 3 inch
(+1.00 m)
+3 ft 3 inch
(+1.00 m)
+10 inch
(+0.25 m)

Fire safety measures

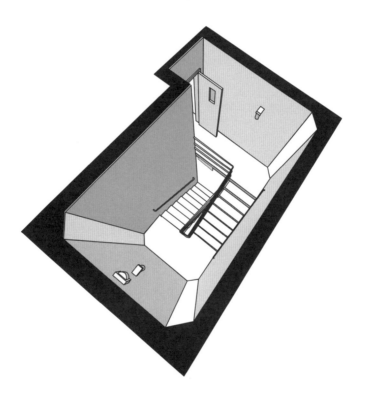

Minimum fire resistance time required of structural elements

Type of building	Cellar		Ground floor and upper floors			
	height over +32 ft 10 inch (+10m)	height up to +32 ft 10 inch (+10m)	height up to +16 ft 5 inch (+5 m)	height up to +65 ft 7 inch (+20m)	height up to +98 ft 5 inch (+30m)	height over +98 ft 5 inch (+30m)
Apartment building	90	60	30[a]	60	90[b]	120[b]
Private house	-	30[a]	30[a]	60	-	-
Institutional buildings[c]	90	60	30[a]	60	90	120[d]
Offices (with fire exting. systems)	60	60	30[a]	30[a]	60	120[d]
(without fire ext. systems)	90	60	30[a]	60	90	X
Shops (with fire exting. systems)	60	60	30[a]	60	60	120[d]
(without fire ext. systems)	90	60	60	60	90	X
Theaters and entertain. buildings (with fire exting. systems)	60	60	30[a]	60	60	120[d]
(without fire ext. systems)	90	60	60	60	90	X
Industrial buildings (with fire exting. systems)	90	60	30[a]	60	60	120[d]
(without fire ext. systems)	120	90	60	90	120	X
Warehouse buildings (with fire exting. systems)	90	60	30[a]	60	90	120[d]
(without fire ext. systems)	120	90	60	90	120	X
Vehicle parking space	90	60	30[a]	60	90	120[d]

a: Plus an additional 60 min. for walls separating different buildings.

b: Reduced to 30 min. for each floor inside a maisonette, as long as this floor does not contribute to the support of the building.

c: Hospitals with various floors have a minimum of 60 minutes.

d: Reduced to 90 minutes for those elements that are not part of the structural system.

X: Not permitted.

Typical fire extinguishing system with sprinklers

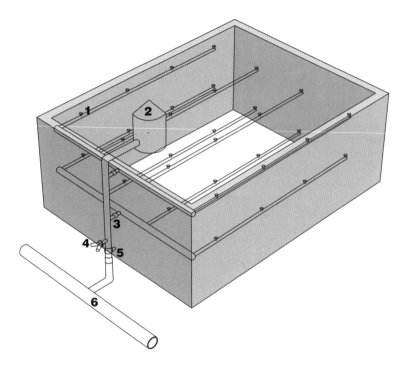

1   Sprinklers. Each sprinkler protects from 8 to 18 m² of floor surface area.

2   Sprinkler system storage tank.

3   Sprinkler system closing valve.

4   Siamese. A twin connection, to which one or two fire engines can be connected.

5   Standpipe closing valve and alarm system. The alarm system is triggered off when water starts to flow through the pipe.

6   Mains water supply.

Fire escape route design: basic principles

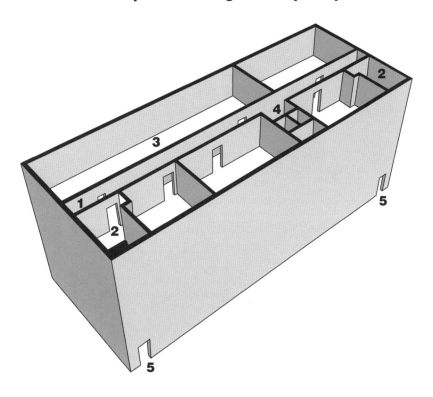

1   Dead-end corridors should not be longer than **+20 ft** *(+6 m)*

2   A stairwell enclosed by fire resistant walls.

3   Large halls require two or more exits.

4   Elevators should not be used as a fire escape route.

5   Stairs must lead directly outside.

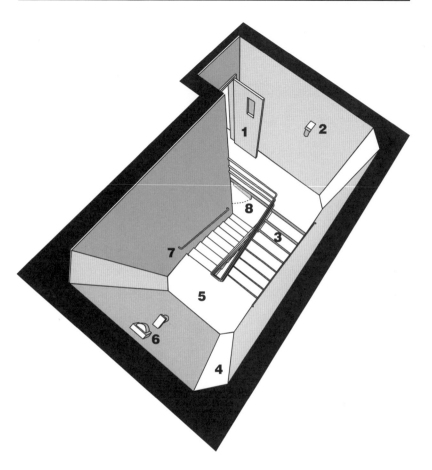

1. Doors must open in the same direction as the escape route.
2. Light signals.
3. A comfortable proportion between steps and risers of the stairs.
4. Rounded corners.
5. The width of the landings must be the same as the stairs.
6. Emergency lighting.
7. The ends of the stair rails must be fixed into the wall.
8. The open door must not interfere with the flow of escape traffic.

Fire escape routes in an apartment building

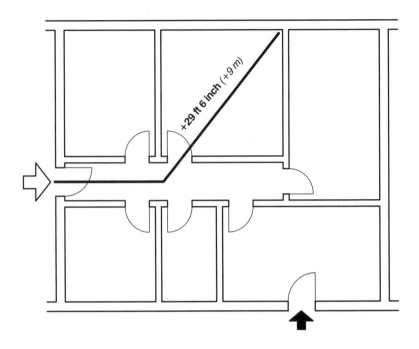

+29 ft 6 inch (+9 m)

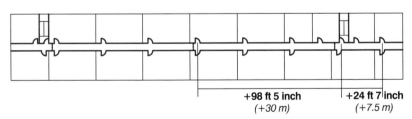

+98 ft 5 inch
(+30 m)

+24 ft 7 inch
(+7.5 m)

⇨ Main door of the apartment

➡ Secondary door of the apartment

⊓ Self closing fire resistant door type FD 30S

| Self closing fire resistant door type FD 20S

Distances in the escape routes in public buildings

Principal use of the building	Maximum distance of a fire escape route:	
	one way	more than one way
Institutional buildings	9	18
Offices	18	45
Commercial buildings and shops	18	45
Indoors commercial centers		
a. at ground level	9	45
b. at upper levels	9	45
Outdoor commercial centers		
a. at ground level	25	no limit
b. at upper levels	9	45
Entertainment buildings	15	32
Meeting halls		
a. with seating	15	32 (2)
b. without seating	18	45 (3)
Industrial buildings (1)	25	45
Storage spaces	18	45
Especially dangerous spaces	9	18
Factories		
a. distance inside the space	9	35
b. total indoor distance	18	45
c. Total outdoor distance	60	100

(1) The distances in industrial buildings depend on the danger level. Here a normal "normal danger level" is assumed.

(2) This can include up to 15 meters in one way.

(3) This can include up to 18 meters in one way.

Principal use of the building	Maximum distance of a fire escape route:	
	one way	more than one way
Institutional buildings	+86 ft 5 inch	+59 ft
Offices	+59 ft	+147 ft 8 inch
Commercial buildings and shops	+59 ft	+147 ft 8 inch
Indoors commercial centers		
a. at ground level	+86 ft 5 inch	+147 ft 8 inch
b. at upper levels	+86 ft 5 inch	+147 ft 8 inch
Outdoor commercial centers		
a. at ground level	+82 ft	no limit
b. at upper levels	+86 ft 5 inch	+147 ft 8 inch
Entertainment buildings	+49 ft 3 inch	+104 ft 12 inch
Meeting halls		
a. with seating	+49 ft 3 inch	+104 ft 12 inch (2)
b. without seating	+59 ft	+147 ft 8 inch (3)
Industrial buildings (1)	+82 ft	+147 ft 8 inch
Storage spaces	+59 ft	+147 ft 8 inch
Especially dangerous spaces	+86 ft 5 inch	+59 ft
Factories		
a. distance inside the space	+86 ft 5 inch	+114 ft 10 inch
b. total indoor distance	+59 ft	+147 ft 8 inch
c. Total outdoor distance	+196 ft 10 inch	+328 ft 1 inch

Determining the different escape routes

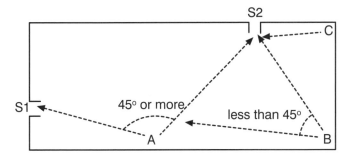

Point A has two alternative routes because angle S1AS2 is 45° or more. Point B hasn't got two alternative routes because angle S1BS2 is less than 45°. point C also has only one route.

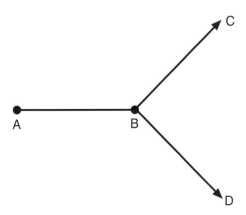

If the escape route starts at point A and separates in two at point B, ángle CBD must have a minimum width of 45° + 2.5° for each additional meter between A and B. (In the previous case in which the routes separate at the starting point, distance AB is considered equal to 0.)

Stairs and elevators

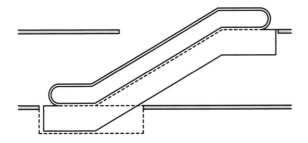

Slope of different types of stairs

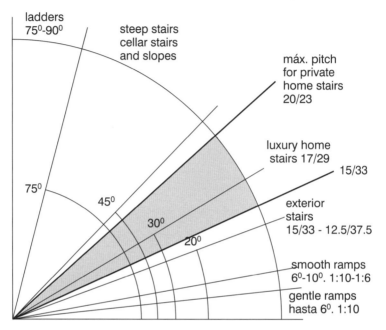

ladders
75⁰-90⁰

steep stairs
cellar stairs
and slopes

máx. pitch
for private
home stairs
20/23

luxury home
stairs 17/29

15/33

75⁰

45⁰

exterior
stairs
15/33 - 12.5/37.5

30⁰

20⁰

smooth ramps
6⁰-10⁰. 1:10-1:6

gentle ramps
hasta 6⁰. 1:10

Width of stairs

Available walking space between the wall surface and the edge of the stair rail or between the stair rails:

< +2 ft 7 inch *(+0.8 m)*: rarely used stairs
> +2 ft 7 inch *(+0.8 m)*: private home stairs
> +2 ft 11 inch *(+0.9 m)*: in buildings of less than three floors
> +3 ft 3 inch *(+1.00 m)*: in multi-family buildings with more than two floors
> +6 ft 5 inch *(+1.25 m)*: in high buildings
wider: if there are more than 150 users

In stairways over +13 ft 1 inch *(+4 m)* wide a central stair rail is installed. In winding stairs the stair rail is installed on the exterior.

dimensions of stairs

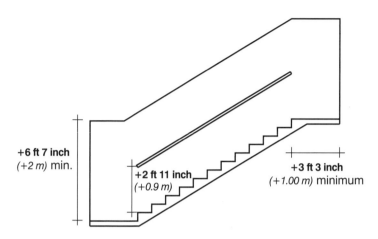

+6 ft 7 inch
(+2 m) min.

+2 ft 11 inch
(+0.9 m)

+3 ft 3 inch
(+1.00 m) minimum

The optimum dimension for risers and steps is 17/29.
2 risers + 1 step = **+2 ft** *(+0.63 m)* approx.

Stairways up to 5 steps do not need a stairrail

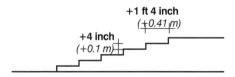

+1 ft 4 inch
(+0.41 m)

+4 inch
(+0.1 m)

Stairways with pitch less than 1:4 do not need a stairrail

Dimensions of elevators

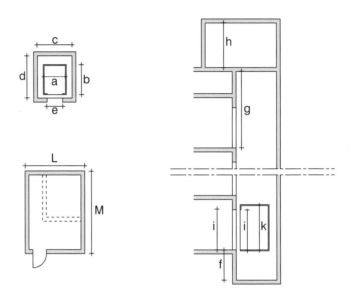

Light elevators for passengers

	load capacity (kg)	400			630				1000			
	speed (m/s)	0.6	1.0	1.6	0.6	1.0	1.6	2.5	0.6	1.0	1.6	2.5
car	a. car width	110			110				110			
	b. car depth	95			140				210			
	k. car height	220			220				220			
door	e. door width	80			80				80			
	i. door height	200			200				200			
shaft	c. shaft width	180			180				180			
	d. car depth	150			210				260			
	f. elevator pit depth	140	150	170	140	150	170	280	140	150	170	280
	g. box height	370	380	400	370	380	400	500	370	380	400	500
engine room	L. engine room width	240			270		300		270		300	
	M. engine room depth	320			370				420			
	h. engine room height	200			200		260		200		260	

Passenger elevators in public buildings (wheelchair accessible)

	load capacity (kg)	800 (10 per.)				1000 (13 per.)				1600 (21 per.)			
	speed (m/s)	0.6	1.0	1.6	2.5	0.6	1.0	1.6	2.5	0.6	1.0	1.6	2.5
car	a. car width	135				150				195			
	b. car depth	140				140				175			
	k. car height	220				230				230			
door	e. door width	80				110				110			
	i. door height	200				210				210			
shaft	c. shaft width	190				240				260			
	d. shaft depth	230				230				260			
	f. elevator pit depth	140	150	170	280	140	150	170	280	140	150	170	280
	g. box height	380		400	500	420			520	440			540
engine room	L. engine room width	250			280	320				320			
	M. engine room depth	370			490	490				550			
	h. engine room height	220			280	240			280	280			

Elevators for hospital trolleys

	load capacity (kg)	1600				2000				2500			
	speed (m/s)	0.6	1.0	1.6	2.5	0.6	1.0	1.6	2.5	0.6	1.0	1.6	2.5
car	a. elevator car width	140				150				180			
	b. elevator car depth	240				270				270			
	k. elevator car height	230				230				230			
door	e. door width	130				130				130			
	i. door height	210				210				210			
shaft	c. shaft width	240				240				270			
	d. shaft depth	230				230				260			
	f. elevator pit depth	170	180	190	280	160	170	190	280	180	190	210	300
	g. box height	440			540	440			540	480			560
engine room	L. engine room width	320				320				350			
	M. engine room depth	550				580				580			
	h. engine room height	280				280				280			

Typical escalator

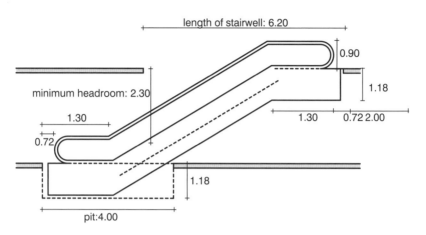

length of stairwell: 6.20

0.90

minimum headroom: 2.30

1.18

1.30

1.30   0.72 2.00

0.72

1.18

pit: 4.00

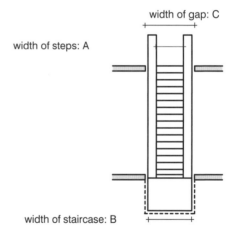

width of gap: C

width of steps: A

width of staircase: B

width of steps	600	800	1000
A	605 - 620	805 - 820	1005 - 1020
B	1170 - 1220	1320 - 1420	1570 - 1620
C	1280	1480	1680
work/hour	5000 - 6000	7000 - 8000	8000 - 10000

Pools
Children's playground

Types of pool construction

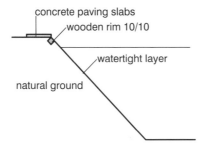

Pool with sloped sides, watertight layer and wooden rim

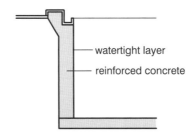

Basic reinforced concrete pool construction

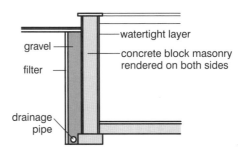

Basic masonry pool with draiange

Pools can also be constructed with polyester. Made of prefabricated elements, they are not self supporting and require a base of solid concrete.

Types of slides

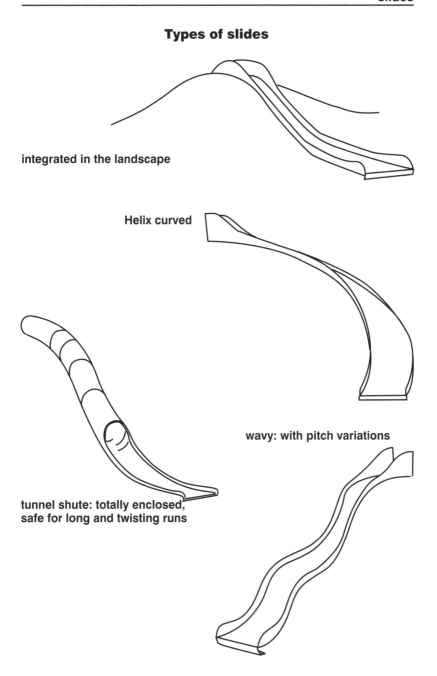

integrated in the landscape

Helix curved

wavy: with pitch variations

tunnel shute: totally enclosed,
safe for long and twisting runs

Parts of a slide

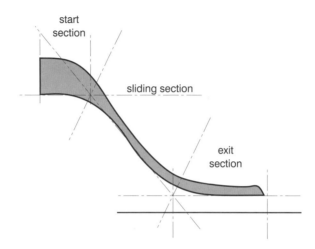

The start section should have the same width as the sliding section and there should be no discontinuity between them.
The final edge of the exit section should be rounded.

Dimensions of a slide

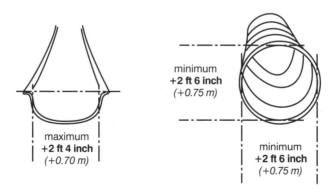

Types of swings

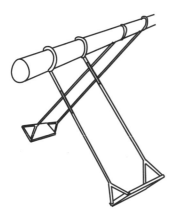

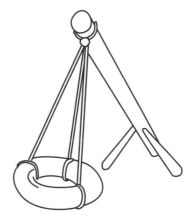

With two suspension points and a rotation axe

With one suspension point: permits multiple use

Swing design

The impact area must remain free of obstacles and have an impact absorbing surface. This area extends 1.50 m from all points where there is potential danger of falling in all possible games.

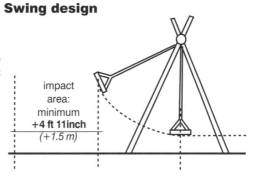

impact area: minimum **+4 ft 11inch** (+1.5 m)

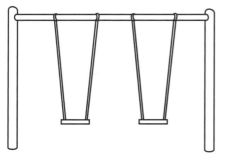

The seats of swings should not hold more than one passenger at a time. Each swing bar should not carry more than two swings.

Structure

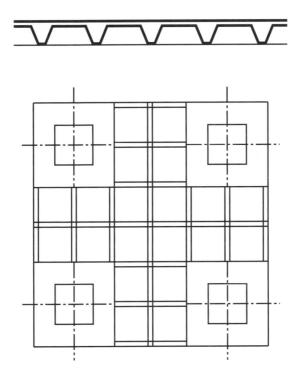

Masonry - vertical supports

items	vertical and horizontal sections	typical height (h)	h/d between lateral supports	critical factors	comments
masonry pillars		+3 ft 3 inch - 13 ft 1inch (+1.00-4 m)	15-20	buckling and compression h/d >6 compression h/d <6 bending	h is the distance between the lateral supports, and d is the thickness of the pillar.
masonry walls		+3 ft 3 inch - 16 ft 5 inch (+1.00-5 m)	18-22	buckling and compression h/d >6 compression h/d <6 bending	h is the distance between the horizontal lateral supports. The wall may also have vertical supports.
walls or pillars of reinforced masonry		+6 ft 7 inch - 22 ft 12 inch (+2-7 m)	20-35	bending	h is the distance between the horizontal lateral supports. The wall may also have vertical supports.

Masonry - floors

items	floor plan and section	typical thickness (d)	span (L)	typical L/d	critical factors comments
masonry arches		+2 inch - 9 inch (+0.05-0.23m)	+6 ft 7 inch - 16 ft 5 inch (+2-5 m)	20-30	bending or cracking at the joints. The fill in the gaps above the arch helps its pretension. L/h between10 -20
reinforced masonry beams		+12 inch - 1 ft 12 inch (+0.3-0.6 m)	+13 ft 1 inch- 39 ft 4 inch (+4-12 m)	12-16	Deflection and cracking at the joints. Deflection.

masonry - roofs

items	sections and floor plans	typical thickness (d)	span (L)	typical L/d	critical factors and comments
masonry shells		+3 inch - 5inch (+0.075-0.13 m)	+19 ft 8inch - 49 ft 3inch (+6-15 m)	80 - 120	Deflection on the edge of the shell. The shell has a funicular form to reduce the tension and the shearing stress. Wider spans may require reinforcement.
masonry arches		+3 inch - 1 ft 12inch (+0.07-0.6 m)	+26 ft 3 inch - 164 ft (+8-50m)	30 - 60	Deflection or cracking. The arch should have a funicular form. Flat arches tend to develop great lateral forces. L/h approximately 5.
masonry vaults		+2 inch - 6 inch (+0.05-0.15 m)	+16 ft 5 inch - 13 ft 3 inch (+5-40m)	30 - 80	Vaults have been constructed with spans up to 13 ft 3 inch (+40 m). Vaults constructed some height from the ground require buttresses to absorb the lateral forces.

Wood - vertical supports

items	vertical and horizontal sections	typical height (h)	h/d between lateral supports	critical factors	comments
pillar of laminated wood		6 ft 7 inch - 13 ft 1 inch (2-4 m)	15 - 30	Breaking, compression h/d < 15 Compression,buckling h/d > 15	w/d = 2 -3 Pillars rising more than one floor may require a reduced h/d.
stud wall		6 ft 7 inch - 13 ft 1 inch (2-4 m)	20 - 35	Compression and bending. The thickness of the insulation must be added on.	Posts are placed at a distance of 400 mm from center to center, and the boards are fixed onto them.
pillar of solid wood		6 ft 7 inch - 13 ft 1 inch (2-4 m)	15 - 30	warping or distortion of wood.	Pillars rising more than one floor may require a reduced h/d.

Wood - floors

items	floor plans and sections	typical thickness (d)	span (L)	typical L/d	critical factors comments
particle board chip board		0.4 inch - 1 inch (12-30 mm)	12 inch - 1 ft 2 inch (0.3-0.6 m)	24	Resistance. Plastic deformation - deflection.
plywood		0.4 inch - 1 inch (12-30 mm)	12 inch - 2 ft 11 inch (0.3-0.9 m)	30 - 40	Resistance. deflection. Concentrated loads

Wood - floors

items	sections and floor plans	typical thickness (d)	span (L)	typical L/d	critical factors comments
soft wood composition boards		1 inch - 1 inch (16-25 mm)	1 ft 12 inch - 2 ft 7 inch 0.6-0.8 m)	25 - 35	Resistance. Deflection.
laminated wood beams: softwood hardwood		8 inch - 12 inch (200-300 mm) 4 inch - 10 inch (100-250 mm)	6 ft 7 inch - 19 ft 8 inch (2-6 m) 6 ft 7 inch - 22 ft 12 inch (2-7 m)	12 - 20 22 - 28	Deflection. Distance between beams 1 ft 6 inch - 1 ft 12 inch (450 - 600 mm).
glued laminated wooden beam		7 inch - 4ft 7 inch (180-1400 mm)	16 ft 5 inch - 39 ft 4 inch 5-12 m)	14 - 18	Deflection. d/b = 3 -5 to avoid instability of that section
wooden beam with open steel web		1 ft 8 inch - 6ft 7 inch (500-2000 mm)	16 ft 5 inch - 59 ft 5-18 m)	8 - 10	Deflection. Vibration.

wood - roofs

items	elevations and sections	typical thickness (d)	span (L)	typical L/d	critical factors, comments
roof decking with boards		1 inch - 3 inch (25-75 mm)	6 ft 7 inch - 20 ft (2-6 m)	45 - 60	Deflection. It is assumed that the decking boards merely rest upon the frame.
roof sheathing with plywood		94 inch - 1 inch (10-20 mm)	12 inch - 3 ft 11 inch (0.3-1.2 m)	50 - 70	Deflection. It is assumed that the surface is continuous.
roof sheathing plywood panels		4 inch - 1 ft 6 inch (100-450 mm)	19 ft 10 inch - 22 ft 12 inch (3-7 m)	30 - 35	Deflection. It is assumed that the panels merely rest upon the frame. a = 12 inch - 1 ft 8 inch (300 - 500 mm).
wooden slat chanelled roof		9 inch - 1 ft 4 inch (225-400 mm)	16 ft 5 inch - 39 ft 4 inch (5-12 m)	25 - 30	It is assumed that the boards merely rest upon the frame.
beams decked with: soft wood hardwood		4 inch - 9 inch (100-225 mm) 4 inch - 10 inch (100-250 mm)	6 ft 7 inch - 20 ft (2-6 m) 9 ft 10 inch - 26 ft 3 inch (3-8 m)	20 - 25 30 - 35	Deflection. It is assumed that the beams merely rest on the supports. Distance between beams: 1 ft 12 inch (600 mm).

Wood - roofs

item	sections and elevations	typical thickness (d)	span (L)	typical L/d	critical factors comments
chords of: softwood hardwood		6 inch - 12 inch (150-300 mm) 8 inch - 1 ft 4 inch (200-400 mm)	6 ft 7 inch - 20 ft (2-6 m) 9 ft 10 inch - 26 ft 3 inch (3-8 m)	10 - 14 15 - 20	Available wood sizes. Resistance to bending. It is assumed that the chords are simply rested on the supports and carry a **6 ft 7 inch** (2 m) width of roof.
beams of glued lamin--ated wood		7 inch - 4 ft 7 inch (180-1400 mm)	13 ft 1 inch - 98 ft 5 inch (4-30 m)	15 - 20	Deflection. It is assumed that the chords simply rest on the supports. Distance between supports: L/910" - L/165" (L/3m - L/5m). d/b = 5 - 8.
box-beams of glued wood		8 inch - 6 ft 7 inch (200-2000 mm)	20 ft - 65 ft 7 inch (6-20 m)	10 - 15	Deflection. Resistance to bending. Horizontal shearing stress. Web buckling. It is assumed that the chords are simply rested on the supports.

Wood - roofs

items	elevations and sections	typical density (d)	span (L)	typical L/d	critical factors comments
open web beam with wooden flanges and steel bars		1 ft 8 inch - 6 ft 7 inch (0.5-2 m)	29 ft 6 inch - 98 ft 5 inch (9-30 m)	10 - 15	The flanges and the web are joined with bolts.
two-pitched trussed rafter frame, without chords		3 ft 11 inch - 6 ft 7 inch (1-2 m)	20 ft - 32 ft 10 inch (6-10 m)	4 - 6	Resistance of the joints. Bending of the joists. Distance 1 ft 12 inch (600 mm).
two-pitched trussed rafter frame, with chords		3 ft 3 inch - 9 ft 10 inch (1-3 m)	20 ft - 65 ft 7 inch (6-20 m)	5 - 7	Resistance of the joints. Distance 6 ft 7 inch - 16 ft 5 inch (2 - 5 m).
parallel chord wooden truss		4 ft 11 inch - 9 ft 10 inch (1.5-3 m)	39 ft 4 inch - 82 ft (12-25 m)	8 - 10	Resistance of the joints. Distance 13 ft 1 inch - 20 ft (4 - 6 m).

Wood - roofs

items	section and floor plans	span (L)	typical L/d	comments
roofing of folded panels		29 ft 6 inch - 65 ft 7 inch (9-20 m)	8 - 15	The panels have two layers w/d = 20 - 30 and 3 inch - 8 inch (75 - 200 mm) thick.
hiperbolic paraboloid roof of three-layered roofing panels		39 ft 4 inch - 98 ft 5 inch (12-30 m)	2 - 8	The shell has two beams at the edges with L/d = 60 -80.
barrel vault roof of three-layered roofing panels		29 ft 6 inch - 98 ft 5 inch (9-30 m)	4 - 8	The panels have two layers. w/d = 2 - 4.
pyramid-like roof		39 ft 4 inch - 114 ft 10 inch (12-35 m)	2 - 6	Simple construction. Steel tension elements are often used at the base.

wood - roofs

Wood - roofs

items	section and floor plans	span (L)	typical L/d	comments
vault of glued laminated wood		39 ft 4 inch - 328 ft 1 inch (12-100 m)	5 - 7	The elements of the vault have a configuration of radial or laminated curves when projected on the plane
laminated roofing		49 ft 3 inch - 82 ft (15-25 m)	5 - 7	The elements in two crossed laminated lines have a configuration of rhomboids when projected on the plane.
hyperbolic paraboloid web structure		39 ft 4 inch - 262 ft 6 inch (12-80 m)	5 - 10	The web is covered with laminated wooden panels. L/d = 60 - 80.
vaulted shell web structure		39 ft 4 inch - 98 ft 15 inch (12-30 m)	5 - 7	The elements of the web must be flexible enough to form the curve. The curve must be approximately a funicular curve.

106

Wood - frame and wall systems

items	section and floor plan	span (L)	typical L/d	comments
rigid frame of glued lamin--ated wood		39 ft 4 inch - 114 ft 10 inch *(12-35 m)*	30 - 50	Distance between frames 13 ft 1 inch - 20 ft *(4 - 6 m)*. The frame may be curved but the cost will increase. L/h = 5 - 7
risers and beam of glued laminated wood		13 ft 1 inch - 98 ft 5 inch *(4-30 m)*	18 - 22	The frame is not rigid and requires diagonal bracing.
rigid frame		29 ft 6 inch - 147 ft 8 inch *(9-45 m)*	20 - 40	The beams are of solid wood and are nailed and glued to the risers. Distance between frames 13 ft 1 inch - 20 ft *(4 - 6 m)*.

Wood - systems of frames and walls

items	section and floor plan	span (L)	typical L/d	comments
arch of glued laminated wood		49 ft 3 inch - 328 ft 1 inch *(15-100 m)*	30 - 50	The maximum length for transportable items is **49 ft 3 inch - 82 ft** *(15 - 25 m)*. The curve must have a funicular form to carry large loads. The floor plan may be square or rectangular. L/h = 5 - 7
floors and walls of plywood		h = **from 2 to 4 floors**		Constructed like a platform structure, in which the vertical elements are not continuous.
braced wooden frame		h = **from 2 to 4 floors**		The frames must have diagonal steel bracing or plywood panels to be rigid.

Concrete - vertical supports

items	vertical and horizontal sections	typical height (h)	h/d between lateral supports	critical factors	comments
pillar constructed on site: - one floor - several floors		6 ft 7 inch - 26 ft 3 inch (2-8 m) 6 ft 7 inch - 13 ft 1 inch (2-4 m)	12 - 18 6 - 15	Buckling and compression h/d >10 Compression h/d <10 Bending	Pillars attached with rigid joints to the beams form frames which function as vertical bracing
wall constructed on site		6 ft 7 inch - 13 ft 1 inch (2-4 m)	18 - 25	Buckling. Construction methods.	
rough concrete wall costructed on site		6 ft 7 inch - 9 ft 10 inch (2-3 m)	10 - 15	Compression	Much used in the construction of apartment blocks. d > 200 mm.
prefabricated pillar - one floor - several floors		6 ft 7 inch - 26 ft 3 inch (2-8 m) 6 ft 7 inch - 13 ft 1 inch (2-4 m)	15 - 30 6 - 20	Buckling and compression h/d >10 Compression h/d <10 Bending. Joints.	Prefabricated products are available with various types of finish.

Concrete - vertical supports

items	vertical and horizontal sections	typical height (h)	h/d between lateral supports	critical factors	comments
load-bearing prefabricated panel		6 ft 7 inch - 9 ft 10 inch (2-3 m)	20 - 25	Buckling. Joints. Construction stress	
prefabricated panel with buttresses		13 ft 1 inch - 26 ft 3 inch (4-8 m)	15 - 25	Erection stress	
pretensed concrete pillar - one floor - several floors		13 ft 1 inch - 26 ft 3 inch (4-8 m) 6 ft 7 inch - 13 ft 1 inch (2-4 m)	15 - 25 10 - 20	Buckling	The pre-tensioning helps to eliminate the traction stresses generated by bending.
pretensed concrete bracing		3 ft 3 inch - 131 ft 2 inch (1-40 m)	1 - 150	Load variations.	More rigid and resistant to corrosion than steel bracing.

Concrete - floors

items	cross sections and floor plans	typical thickness (d)	span (L)	typical L/d	critical factors comments
solid unidirectional slab - reinforced - pretensed		4 inch - 10 inch *(100-250 mm)* 5 inch - 8 inch *(125-200 mm)*	6 ft 7 inch - 22 ft 12 inch *(2-7 m)* 16 ft 5 inch - 29 ft 6 inch *(5-9 m)*	22 - 32 38 - 45	Deflection. Bending. The tiles that are simply rested have the lower L/d values.
bidirectional reinforced slab		4 inch - 10 inch *(100-250 mm)*	20 ft - 36 ft *(6-11 m)*	28 - 35	Deflection. Bending. Adequate for large and concentrated loads. $L < L1 < 1.4\ L$.
unidirectional ribbed slab -reinforced - pretensed		1 ft 2 inch - 2 ft 2 inch *(350-650 mm)* 1 ft 6 inch - 2 ft 2 inch *(450-650 mm)*	13 ft 1 inch - 39 ft 4 inch *(4-12 m)* 32 ft 10 inch - 59 ft *(10-18 m)*	18 - 26 30 - 38	Deflection. Bending. Cutting. More adequate for wide spans with small loads. a, b and c as in the next.

Concrete - floors

items	cross sections and floor plans	typical thickness (d)	span (L)	typical L/d	critical factors comments
waffle slab - reinforced - pretensed		1 ft 2 inch - 2 ft 2 inch (350-650 mm) 1 ft 6 inch - 2 ft 2 inch (450-650 mm)	29 ft 6 inch - 49 ft 3 inch (9-15 m) 32 ft 10 inch - 72 ft 2 inch (10-22m)	18 - 24 30 - 38	Deflection. Bending. Casts are available in set sizes. More costly than a ribbed slab. Dimensions: a = 100-200 mm b = 900-1800 mm c = 60 - 100 mm.
one way beam reinforced with empty blocks		6 inch - 12 inch (150-300 mm)	9 ft 10 inch - 22 ft 12 inch (3-7 m)	20 - 25	Bending. Cutting. Small holes are easy to make through which conduits can be passed.
partly pretensed ribbed slab		12 inch - 1 ft 8 inch (300-500 mm)	32 ft 10 inch - 49 ft 3 inch (10-15m)	35 - 40	Deflection. Bending. There is less upward creep and deflection than in totally pretensed slabs.

Concrete - floors

items	cross sections and floor plans	typical thickness (d)	span (L)	typical L/d	critical factors comments
floor of pretensed beams and blocks		6 inch - 8 inch (150-200 mm)	9 ft 10 inch - 22 ft 12 inch (3-7 m)	30 - 35	Bending. Drift. The beams and blocks are prefabricated but support a cast-in-situ layer 2 inch - 3 inch (50 - 75 mm) thick.
prefabricated pretensed board		4 inch - 8 inch (100-200 mm)	20 ft - 29 ft 6 inch (6-9 m)	35 - 45	Drift caused by movable loads. Bending. Slabs thicker than 7 inch (175 mm) are often manufactured with hollow core. Thickness of the finish surface a = 2 inch - 3 inch (50 - 75 mm).
pretensed hollow core slab		4 inch - 1 ft 2 inch (100-350 mm)	20 ft - 32 ft 10 inch (6-10 m)	35 - 40	Bending. The beams are prefabricat but carry a layer cast on site, aprox. 1 inch - 2 inch (35 - 50 mm) thick.
large span slab - reinforced - pretensed		4 inch - 12 inch (100-300 mm) 4 inch - 9 inch (100-225 mm)	9 ft 10 inch - 22 ft 12 inch (3-7 m) 13 ft 1 inch - 29 ft 6 inch (4-9 m)	26 - 32 35 - 45	Bending. Drift. The slab is prefabricat but carries a layer cast on site. The slab often requires support during construction.

113

Concrete - floors

items	cross sections and floor plans	typical thickness (d)	span (L)	typical L/d	critical factors comments
prefabricated pretensed double-T beams		1 ft 2 inch - 2 ft 7 inch (350-800 mm)	29 ft 6 inch - 59 ft (9-18 m)	20 - 30	Live load. Bending. Shearing. Construction stress. The beams support a cast on site slab of approx. **2 inch - 3 inch** (50 - 75 mm) thickness.
flat slab without abacus - reinforced - pretensada		**5 inch - 8 inch** (125-200 mm) **8 inch - 9 inch** (200-225 mm)	**13 ft 1 inch - 26 ft 3 inch** (4-8 m) **29 ft 6 inch - 32 ft 10 inch** (9-10 m)	**28 - 36** **40 - 48**	Drift. Bending. Shearing around the pillars. Compared to a beam and slab construction flat slabs are less thick and the casts are cheaper, but less resistant to lateral forces.
flat slab with abacus - reinforced - pretensed		**5 inch - 12 inch** (125-300 mm) **8 inch - 9 inch** (200-225 mm)	**16 ft 5 inch - 32 ft 10 inch** (5-10 m) **39 ft 4 inch - 131 ft 3 inch** (12-40 m)	**28 - 36** **40 - 48**	Drift. Bending. Shearing around the pillars. a = 1,25d - 1,45d b = **L/9 ft 10"** (3 m)

Concrete - floors

items	cross sections and floor plans	typical thickness (d)	span (L)	typical L/d	critical factors comments
T or L beams - reinforced - pretensed		1 ft 4 inch - 2 ft 4 inch (400-700mm) 12 inch - 2 ft 9 inch (300-850 mm)	16 ft 5 inch - 49 ft 3 inch (5-15 m) 29 ft 6 inch - 78 ft 9 inch (9-24 m)	14 - 20 20 - 30	The distance between beams is **9ft 10 inch - 22 ft 11 inch** *(3 - 7 m)* and the slab's thickness is **4 inch - 7 inch** *(100 - 175 mm)*. The beams that are simply rested have smaller L/d values.
wide beam - reinforced - pretensed		1 ft 2 inch - 2 ft 2 inch (350-650 mm) 12 inch - 1 ft 8 inch (300-500 mm)	20 ft - 32 ft 10 inch (39-4 m) 29 ft 6 inch - 49 ft 3 inch (9-15 m)	16 - 22 22 - 32	Drift. Bending. Used when the height of the space is limited. The beams that are simply rested have the lowest L/d values. a = **1 ft 12 inch - 3 ft 11 inch** *(600 - 1200 mm)*.

concrete - roofs

items	cross sections and floor plans	typical thickness (d)	span (L)	typical L/d	critical factors comments
one-way solid reinforced slab		5 inch - 1 ft 8 inch (125-500 mm)	9 ft 10 inch - 20 ft (3-6 m)	20 - 30	Drift. Bending.
ribbed reinforced slab		1 ft 8 inch - 3 ft 11 inch (500-1200 mm)	20 ft - 45 ft 11 inch (6-14 m)	25 - 30	Drift. Bending. Shearing a = **4 inch - 6 inch** (100 - 150 mm) c = **2 inch - 4 inch** (50 - 100 mm)
slab with reticular reinforcement		2 ft 1 inch - 4 ft 11 inch (625-1500 mm)	29 ft 6 inch - 52 ft 6 inch (9-16 m)	20 - 25	Drift. Bending. Dimensions as previous one.

concrete - roofs

items	cross sections and floor plans	typical thickness (d)	span (L)	typical L/d	critical factors comments
flat slab reinforced without abacus		1 ft 4 inch - 2 ft 11 inch *(400-900 mm)*	13 ft 1 inch - 26 ft 3 inch *(4-8 m)*	32	Drift. Bending. Shearing around the pillars.
hollow core slab pretensed		4 inch - 8 inch *(100-200 mm)*	20 ft - 32 ft 10 inch *(6-10 m)*	40 - 50	Resistance to compression of the unit. Variations in the live load. The slabs are prefabricated but carry a **2 inch - 3 inch** *(50 - 75 mm)*. surface cast on site.
pretensed double T beams		1 ft 2 inch - 2 ft 7 inch *(350-800 mm)*	39 ft 4 inch - 82 ft *(12-25 m)*	30 - 35	Drift. Bending. Construction stress.
pretensed single T beams		2 ft 6 inch - 8 ft 2 inch *(750-2500 mm)*	49 ft 3 inch - 82 ft *(15-25 m)*	30 - 35	Drift. Bending. Construction stress. The beams are prefabricated but carry a **2 inch - 3 inch** *(50 - 75 mm)*. surface cast on site.

Concrete - roofs

items	cross sections and floor plans	typical thickness (d)	span (L)	typical L/d	critical factors comments
slab of reinforced lightweight concrete		4 inch - 8 inch (100-200mm)	6 ft 7 inch - 16 ft 5 inch (2-5 m)	20 - 25	Bending. The slabs are connected with lines of reinforced concrete cast on site.
reinforced inverted hyperbolic paraboloid (umbrella)		3 inch - 4 inch (75-100mm)	29 ft 6 inch - 49 ft 3 inch (9-15 m)	120 - 200	Tension reinforcement is required at the vertex of the umbrella. The umbrellas are independent and may be at different heights. L/h = 6 - 12
hyperbolic paraboloid reinforced shell		3 inch - 4 inch (75-100mm)	49 ft 3 inch - 180 ft 5 inch (15-55 m)	200 - 450	Drift at the vertexes. The beams at the edges may be pretensed to bear the tension stresses. L/h = 4 - 7
vault		3 inch - 12 inch (75-300mm)	49 ft 3 inch - 393 ft 8 inch (15-120 m)	300 - 450	Buckling of the shell. Minimum d = **2 inch** (60 mm). The ring or belt around the base may be pretensed.

Concrete - roofs

items	cuts and floor plans	typical thickness (d)	span (L)	typical L/d	critical factors comments
folded reinforced slab		**3 inch - 5 inch** (75-125 mm)	**29 ft 6 inch - 118 ft 1 inch** (9-36 m)	**40 - 50 w/d**	Bending of the slab. Connection load at a valley. d minimum **2 inch** (60 mm). L/h = 8 - 15.
cylindrical reinforced slab		**3 inch - 4 inch** (75-100 mm)	**82 ft - 131 ft 3 inch** (25-40 m)	**50 - 65 w/d**	d minimum **2 inch** (60 mm). The slab may be pretensed to support tension stresses. L/h = 10 - 15
oblique reinforced network		**12 inch - 2 ft 4 inch** (300-700 mm)	**32 ft 10 inch - 65 ft 7 inch** (10-20 m)	25 - 35	Drift. Bending. The corners are more rigid with an oblique reticule, thus permitting a wider span.

Concrete - frames

items	cuts and floor plans	span (L)	typical L/d	critical factors comments
prefabricated single floor frames		39 ft 4 inch - 78 ft 9 inch (12-24m)	22 - 30	If a join in the horizontal member is needed, it should be in the corner, or at a distance L74 from the corner.
arches		49 ft 3 inch - 196 ft 10 inch (15-60m)	28 - 40	Normally arches are continuous and totally rigid. L/h = 4-12.
prefabricated exterior frames with interiors cast on site		20 ft - 39 ft 4 inch (6-12m)	22 - 30	The joins between prefabricated members are done with in-situ concrete. Prefabricated members can be used for interior frames. The system is suitable for buildings up to 20 floors high.
system of floors and walls cast on site		20 ft - 39 ft 4 inch (6-12m)	25 - 30	Normally a standard and fast casting system is used. The system is rigid and is used for buildings up to 20 floors high.

Concrete - frames

items	cuts and floor plans	span (L)	typical L/d	critical factors comments
prefabricated system of walls and floors		20 ft - 39 ft 4 inch (6-12m)	22 - 25	Normally there are no rigid connections between the walls and the floor. It is a low cost system that may have up to 15 floors.
prefabricated beams and pillars with prefabricated floors		20 ft - 39 ft 4 inch (6-12m)	14 - 16	With rigid connections the system can only have up to 2 floors without vertical bracing.
frameworks for several floors cast on site		16 ft 5 inch - 49 ft 3 inch (5-15m) floors	1 - 5	Cast on site framework without vertical bracing is a low cost system up to 15 floors.

121

Concrete - frames

items	sections and floor plans	span (L)	typical L/d	critical factors comments
bracing walls or rigid frame structural bracing		32 ft 10 inch - 180 ft 5 inch (10-55 m) floors	4 - 5	The bracing walls interact with the rigid frames to create a vertical bracing system for the whole height of the building. h/w is greater in buildings with less than 20 floors.
tubular framework structure		131 ft 3 inch - 213 ft 3 inch (40-65 m) floors	6 - 7	Called a tube within a tube structure. The tube interacts with the core.
central core structure with suspended floors or semi-rigid framework		32 ft 10 inch - 98 ft 5 inch (10-30 m) floors	8 - 12	The core provides all the lateral stability. The surface of the suspended floors is limited.

steel - vertical supports

items	vertical and horizontal sections	typical height (h)	h/d between lateral supports	critical factors	comments
open profile lamintaed steel - one floor - several floors		6 ft 7 inch - 26 ft 3 inch (2-8 m) / 12 inch - 13 ft 1 inch (2-4 m)	20 - 05 / 7 - 18	Buckling (h/d > 14). Buckling and compression (h/d < 14)	Special profiles can be made to order. Open profiles are easier to join.
closed profile laminted steel - one floor - several floo		6 ft 7 inch - 26 ft 3 inch (2-8 m) / 12 inch - 13 ft 1 inch (2-4 m)	20 - 05 / 7 - 28	Buckling(h/d > 20). Buckling and compression (h/d < 20)	Closed profiles have less exposed surface and more resistance to twisting than open profiles.
trussed pillar		13 ft 1 inch - 32 ft 10 inch (4-10m)	20 - 25	Buckling	Trussing is used when a large pillar is required
steel and concrete composite pillar		12 inch - 13 ft 1 inch (2-4 m)	6 - 15	Buckling y crushing (h/d > 10)	Concrete increases the rigidity and resistance to fire.

steel - vertical supports

items	vertical and horizontal cuts	typical height (h)	h/d between lateral supports	critical factors	comments
Laminated steel pillars with steel panels		6 ft 7 inch - 26 ft 3 inch (2-8 m)	15 - 50	Buckling	Steel pillars may also be used with drywall or plywood.
High reistance tension bars		3 ft 3 inch - 131 ft 3 inch (1-40 m)		Axial rigidity.	Tension bracing may consist of solid bars or of cables. Bars are less resistant to tension but offer greater axial rigidity.

steel - floors

items	cuts	typical thickness (d)	span (L)	typical L/d	critical factors comments
steel floor		2 inch - 3 inch (50-75 mm)	6 ft 7 inch - 9 ft 10 inch (2-3 m)	35 - 40	Drift.
laminated steel floor with concrete finish		4 inch - 6 inch (100-150 mm)	6 ft 7 inch - 13 ft 1 inch (2-4 m)	25 - 30	Drift of the laminated steel when used as the cast. Thickness of concrete in order to be fire resistant. a = 2 inch - 3 inch (40 - 80 mm).
floor supported by "Grey" angle irons		4 inch - 1 ft 8 inch (100-500 mm)	13 ft 1 inch - 39 ft 4 inch (4-12 m)	18 - 28	Drift.
floor supported by deep web beams		8 inch - 1 ft 8 inch (200-500 mm)	20 ft - 98 ft 5 inch (6-30 m)	15 - 20	Drift. Resistance to bending stress.

steel - floors

items	cross sections	typical thickness (d)	span (L)	typical L/d	critical factors comments
laminated steel truss		3 ft 3 inch - 13 ft 1 inch (1-4 m)	39 ft 4 inch - 147 ft 8 inch (12-45 m)	8 - 15	Axial compression of the elements. Joints. Deflection.
Vierendeel truss		3 ft 3 inch - 9 ft 10 inch (1-3 m)	20 ft - 59 ft 1 inch (6-18 m)	4 - 12	Reistance to bending near the supports. Deflection.
compound steel girder		12 inch - 3 ft 3 inch (0.3-1 m)	22 ft 12 inch - 49 ft 3 inch (7-15 m)	20 - 25	Often used combining joists in between the beams. 25 % cheaper than steel regarding the simpler cross-sections.

steel - roofs

items	cross sections	typical thickness (d)	span (L)	typical L/d	critical factors comments
laminated steel panels		1 inch - 5 inch (25-120 mm)	6 ft 7 inch - 20 ft (2-6 m)	40 - 70	Deflection.
steel sandwich panel		3 inch (75 mm)	6 ft 7 inch - 9 ft 10 inch (2-3 m)	25 - 30	The panel has synthetic foam insulation. It is important that the insulation material is well bonded to the metal sheet.
reinforced wood wool		2 inch - 6 inch (50-150 mm)	6 ft 7 inch - 13 ft 1 inch (2-4 m)	20 - 25	Deflection. Resistance.
laminated steel angles		5 inch - 12 inch (120-300 mm)	9 ft 10 inch - 39 ft 4 inch (3-12 m)	25 - 35	Deflection. Sometimes the lower axis is too flexible.

steel - roofs

items	cross sections	typical thickness (d)	span (L)	typical L/d	critical factors comments
laminated steel open web beam		12 inch - 3 ft 3 inch (300-1000 mm)	16 ft 5 inch - 65 ft 7 inch (5-20 m)	15 - 25	Deflection. Buckling.
laminated steel Grey truss		4 inch - 1 ft 8 inch (100-500 mm)	20 ft - 45 ft 11 inch (6-14 m)	20 - 30	Deflection.
deep web S-shaped angle irons		8 inch - 3 ft 3 inch (200-1000 mm)	20 ft - 196 ft 10 inch (6-60 m)	18 - 26	Deflection. Resistance to bending. Buckling of the upper flange.

steel - roofs

items	cross sections	span (L)	typical L/d	critical factors comments
laminated steel open web beam		20 ft - 59 ft 1 inch (6-18 m)	10 - 18	Buckling of the web of a beam. Shearing.
flat truss of laminated steel		39 ft 4 inch - 246 ft 1 inch (12-75 m)	10 - 18	Resistance to bending. Deflection. Distance between trusses 6 - 12 m. Curved truss for spans greater than 25 m.
pitched truss of laminated steel		26 ft 3 inch - 65 ft 7 inch (8-20 m)	5 - 10	The truss may be constructed of steel angle irons bolted together.

steel - roofs

items	cross sections and floor plans	span (L)	typical L/d	critical factors comments
space truss		**98 ft 5 inch - 492 ft 1 inch** *(30-150 m)*	**15 - 30**	A space truss has semi-rigid joints and works like a three-dimensional reticular structure. It may have a triangular, square or hexagonal reticule. $d = 1,4\ h = 5 - 12\ \%\ L$ $L < L1 < 1,4\ L$
trussed barrel vault		**65 ft 7 inch - 328 ft 1 inch** *(20-100 m)*	**55 - 60**	The vault may consist of one or two layers of steel. $L/h = 5 - 6$
undulated barrel vault shell		**98 ft 5 inch - 147 ft 8 inch** *(30-45 m)*	**4 - 5**	Consisting of two undulated layers of laminated steel, joined by bolts and containing a layer of insulation in between.
cable supported beam		**196 ft 10 inch - 492 ft 1 inch** *(60-150 m)*	**5 - 10**	Support of the horizontal members by cables allows for much greater spans.

steel - roofs

steel - roofs

items	cross sections and floor plans	span (L)	typical L/d	critical factors comments
roof surface supported by cables	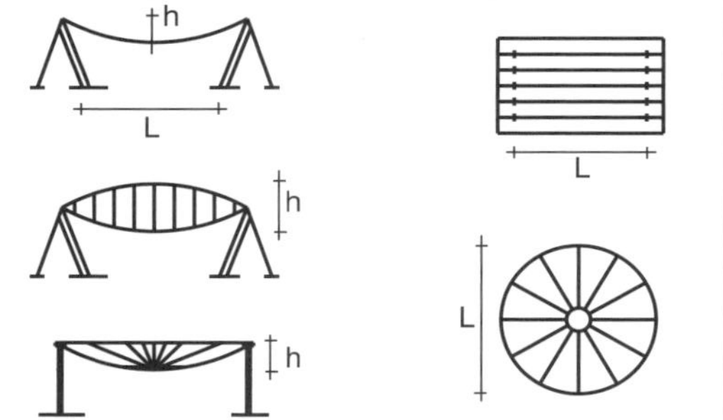	164 ft 1 inch - 590 ft 6 inch (50-180 m)	8 - 15	The roof may consist of a single curve or of a sinclastic double curve.
rigid reticular roof surface	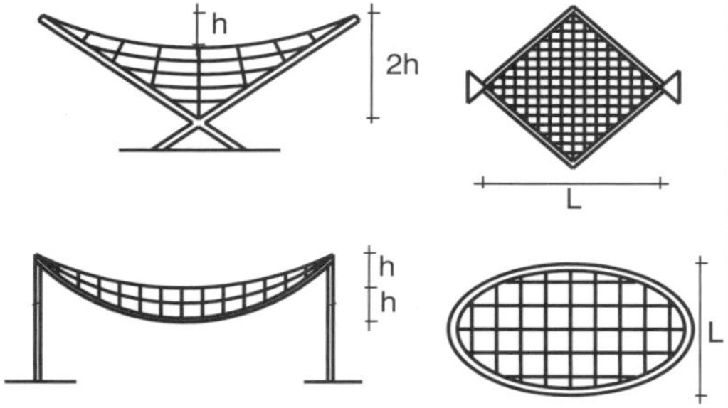	98 ft 5 inch - 590 ft 6 inch (30-180 m)	8 - 15	The roof has a double anticlastic curve.

131

steel - roofs

items	cross sections and floor plans	span (L)	typical L/d	critical factors comments
single shell reticular vault		49 ft 3 inch - 328 ft 1 inch (15-100 m)	5 - 7	Double layer vaults can span gaps up to 200 m wide.
double-layer roof panels		29 ft 6 inch - 98 ft 5 inch (9-30 m)	10 - 20	A single layer construction can span a maximum gap of 25 m. The main problems are the joints and buckling.
double layer hyperbolic paraboloid roof shell		29 ft 6 inch - 98 ft 5 inch (9-30 m)	6 - 12	The steel panels are placed on the straight lines of the curve and curved slightly.
stainless steel membrane supported by air		262 ft 6 inch - 984 ft 3 inch (80-300 m)	25 - 30	A very small L/h is sufficient and produces a nearly flat surface.

steel - frames

items	cross sections and floor plans	span (L)	typical L/d	critical factors comments
one-floor rigid frame		29 ft 6 inch - 196 ft 10 inch (9-60 m)	35 - 40	The frame is rigid within its own plane. The typical distance between frames is: L/4 - L/6.
arch		196 ft 10 inch - 492 ft 1 inch (60-150 m)	40 - 50	Buckling may be critical. The arch has articulated joints at the base and sometimes in the middle. L/h = 5 - 15.
one-floor posts and beam structure		20 ft - 131 ft 3 inch (6-40 m)	12 - 20	The frame is not rigid within its own plane and requires bracing.
rigid frame for several floors		20 ft - 65 ft 7 inch (6-20 m)	20 - 35	Sideway between floors may be critical. Joints between beams and posts must be rigid and require soldering or bolts. It is economical up to 25 floors, and may reach 15 floors without bracing if the joints are rigid.

steel - frames

items	cross sections and floor plans	height (H) (floors)	typical H/W	critical factors comments
simple frames with bracing		5 - 20 floors	6 - 8	There are no rigid joints between the frames and the bracing. The bracing is more efficient if it is vertical bracing and not a rigid frame.
rigid frames with bracing		10 - 40 floors	3 - 4	The joints between the frames and the bracing are rigid.
rigid frames with vertical and horizontal bracing		40 - 60 floors	5 - 7	Horizontal bracing reduces sidesway.

steel - frames

items	cross sections and floor plans	height (H) (floors)	typical	critical factors comments
tubular framework structure		30 - 80 floors	5 - 7	Extra-deep beams and posts offer rigidity so the stucture works like a perforated shell tubular structure.
open web tubular structure		60 - 110 floors	5 - 7	The diagonals support vertical and horizontal loads, supplying rigidity.

Materials

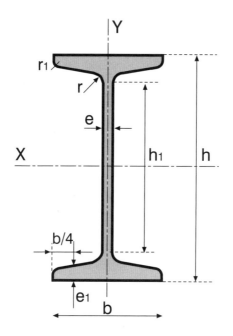

Weight of various materials per m³ or m²

	material	kg/m³	kg/m² - thickness
aggregates	water	1000	
	clay	1925	
	earth	1440	
	cement	1440	
	gravel	1600	
	sand	1600	
	lime mortar	1680	
	quick lime	880	
	concrete	2300	
	concrete, reinforced (2% steel)	2400	
metals	iron, cast	7205	
	iron, wrought	7848	
	steel, sheet		10.20 1.3 mm
	stainless steel, sheet		4.00 0.4 mm
	aluminum, cast	2770	
	brass	8425	
	copper, cast	8730	
	lead, cast	11322	
	lead, sheet		20.40 co.4
	lead, sheet		35.72 co.7
	zinc, cast	6838	
stone	granite	2660	
	marble	2720	
	chalk	2125	
plastering	plaster, light (2 layers)		10,20 13 mm
	plaster, hard (2 layers)		11,60 13 mm
	plaster and lath		29.30
insulation	wood wool		36.60 50 mm
	fiberglass		1.02 100 mm
	cork	80	
	cork, insulation (panels)		6.50 50 mm
	expanded polystyrene, sheet		0.75 50 mm
glass	glass		10.00 4 mm
	glass		15.00 6 mm
	glass		25.00 10 mm

Weight of various materials per ft³ or ft²

	material	lb/ft³	lb/ft² - thickness	
aggregates	water	62.57		
	clay	120.45		
	earth	90.1		
	cement	90.1		
	gravel	100.11		
	sand	100.11		
	lime mortar	105.12		
	quick lime	55.06		
	concrete	143.91		
	concrete, reinforced (2% steel)	150.17		
metals	iron, cast	75.4		
	iron, wrought	491.06		
	steel, sheet		2.09	0.05ft
	stainless steel, sheet		0.82	0.02ft
	aluminum, cast	173.32		
	brass	527.16		
	copper, cast	546.24		
	lead, cast	708.43		
	lead, sheet		78.94	co.4
	lead, sheet		22.54	co.7
	zinc, cast	427.86		
stone	granite	166.44		
	marble	170.19		
	chalk	132.96		
plastering	plaster, light (2 layers)		2.09	0.52ft
	plaster, hard (2 layers)		2.38	0.52ft
	plaster and lath			6.02ft
insulation	wood wool		7.52	2ft
	fiberglass		0.21	4ft
	cork	5		
	cork, insulation (panels)		1.34	2ft
	expanded polystyrene, sheet		0.15	2ft
glass	glass		2.05	0.16ft
	glass		3.08	0.24ft
	glass		5.13	0.4ft

material		kg/m³	kg/m² - thickness
wood	hardwood (oak)	720	
	hardwood (mahogany)	530	
	hardwood (teak)	660	
	hardwood, plank		16,10 23 mm
	softwood (pine, yew)	670	
	softwood (fir)	450	
	softwood (red cedar)	390	
	softwood, floorboard		12.20 6 mm
	laminated wood, sheet		4.10 3,2 mm
sheathing	hardboard (standard)		2.35 3.2 mm
	hardboard (medium)		3.70 6.4 mm
	MDF, sheet		13.80 18 mm
	particle board		14,45 12,5 mm
	calcium silicate board		5,80 6 mm
	drywall		2,20 3 mm
	plasterboard		9,00 9,5 mm
flooring	beaten earth	2080	
	parquet flooring		7.00 15 mm
	linoleum, sheet		4.50 3.2 mm
	vinyl, floor tile		4,00 2 mm
	cork tiling		3.00 3.2 mm
	rubber tiling		5,90 4 mm
	flat cement tile		51,00 4 mm
	flat tile		77,00 100 mm
	terrazzo		34.20 16 mm
	promenade tile (on mortar)		32,00 12.5 mm
roofing	asphalt rolled roofing		47.00 20 mm
	thatch (with the battens)		41.50 300 mm
	aluminum, roofing		3.70 0.8 mm
	copper, roofing		5,70 0,6 mm
	lead, sheet		20.40 co.4
	zinc, roofing		5,70 0,8mm
	pantile		42.00 315 mm
	PVC roofing, sheet		2.50 2 mm
	MDF, sheet		3.80 18 mm
	particle board		14.45 12.5 mm

material		lb/ft³	kg/m² - thickness
wood	hardwood (oak)	11533,29	
	hardwood (mahogany)	8489,78	
	hardwood (teak)	10572,18	
	hardwood, plank		16,10 0.9 inch
	softwood (pine, yew)	10732,37	
	softwood (fir)	7208,31	
	softwood (red cedar)	6247,2	
	softwood, floorboard		12.20 0.24 inch
	laminated wood, sheet		4.10 0.13 inch
sheathing	hardboard (standard)		2.35 0.13 inch
	hardboard (medium)		3.70 0.25 inch
	MDF, sheet		13.80 0.71 inch
	particle board		14,45 0.49 inch
	calcium silicate board		5,80 0.24 inch
	drywall		2,20 0.12 inch
	plasterboard		9,00 0.37 inch
flooring	beaten earth	33318,4	
	parquet flooring		7.00 0.59 inch
	linoleum, sheet		4.50 0.13 inch
	vinyl, floor tile		4,00 0.08 inch
	cork tiling		3.00 0.13 inch
	rubber tiling		5,90 0.16 inch
	flat cement tile		51,00 0.16 inch
	flat tile		77,00 3.94 inch
	terrazzo		34.20 0.63 inch
	promenade tile (on mortar)		32,00 0.49 inch
roofing	asphalt rolled roofing		47.00 0.79 inch
	thatch (with the battens)		41.50 11.81 inch
	aluminum, roofing		3.70 0.03 inch
	copper, roofing		5,70 0.02 inch
	lead, sheet		20.40 co.4
	zinc, roofing		5,70 0.03 inch
	pantile		42.00 1 ft
	PVC roofing, sheet		2.50 0.08 inch
	MDF, sheet		3.80 0.71 inch
	particle board		14.45 0.49 inch

Brick types and denominations	Dimensions (cm)	Weight per unit (kg)	Thickness of the bed (cm)	Units per m³	Mortar per m³	mix design, batching
solid, normal	25 x 12 x 5	3,0	0,5 1,0 1,5	582 534 493	0,140 0,215 0,275	1:5 1:5 1:5
solid, perforated	25 x 12 x 5	2,7	0,5 1,0 1,5	582 534 493	0,225 0,255 0,300	1:5 1:6 1:6
solid, perforated	25 x 12 x 7	3,8	0,5 1,0 1,5	427 400 377	0,200 0,240 0,275	1:5 1:6 1:6
solid, perforated	25 x 12 x 9	4,0	0,5 1,0 1,5	335 320 305	0,190 0,210 0,250	1:5 1:6 1:6

Brick types and denominations	Dimensions (inch)	Weight per unit (lb)	Thickness of the bed (inch)	Units per ft^3	Mortar per ft^3	mix design, batching
solid, normal	9.84 x 4.72 x 1.97	6.63	0,2	20556.24	4.94	1:5
			1,39	18860.88	7.59	1:5
			1,59	17412.75	9.71	1:5
solid, perforated	9.84 x 4.72 x 1.97	5.96	0,2	20556.24	7.94	1:5
			1,39	18860.88	9	1:6
			1,59	17412.75	10.59	1:6
solid, perforated	9.84 x 4.72 x 2.76	8.39	0,2	15081,64	7.06	1:5
			1,39	14128	8.47	1:6
			1,59	13315.64	9.71	1:6
solid, perforated	9.84 x 4.72 x 3.76	8.84	0,2	11832.2	6.71	1:5
			1,39	11302.4	7.41	1:6
			1,59	10772.6	8.83	1:6

Brick types and denominations	Dimensions (cm)	Weight per unit (kg)	Thickness of the bed (cm)	Units per m³	Mortar per m³	mix design, batching
single core hollow brick	25 x 12 x 5	1,5	0,5 1,0 1,5	582 534 493	0,140 0,215 0,275	1:5 1:5 1:5
double core hollow brick	25 x 12 x 7	2,0	0,5 1,0 1,5	335 320 305	0,200 0,225 0,250	1:5 1:5 1:5
treble core hollow brick	25 x 12 x 9	2,5	0,5 1,0 1,5	250 230 210	0,180 0,200 0,240	1:5 1:5 1:5
hollow cladding tile	25 x 12 x 3	1,0	These units are used for building partitions and are fixed with plaster			

Brick types and denominations	Dimensions (inch)	Weight per unit (lb)	Thickness of the bed (inch)	Units per ft³	Mortar per ft³	mix design, batching
single core hollow brick	9.84 x 4.72 x 1.97	3.32	0,2 1,39 1,59	20556.24 18860.88 17412.75	4.94 7.59 7.06	1:5 1:5 1:5
double core hollow brick	9.84 x 4.72 x 2.76	4.42	0,2 1,39 1,59	11832.2 11302.4 10772.6	7.06 7.95 8.83	1:5 1:5 1:5
treble core hollow brick	9.84 x 4.72 x 3.76	5.53	0,2 1,39 1,59	8830 8123.6 7417.2	6.36 7.06 8.48	1:5 1:5 1:5
hollow cladding tile	9.84 x 4.72 x 1.18	2.21	These units are used for building partitions and are fixed with plaster			

Wood	Density	Level of hardness	Type	Characteristics	Applications
Birch	45.1 lb/ft³ (720 kg/m³)	5	soft	Easy to work. Color: white - pale tan.	Carpentry. Easy to bend.
Common fir	28.16 lb/ft³ (450 kg/m³)	4	conifer	Elastic. Color: white. Does not warp.	Masts, furniture scaffolding, shoring.
Cedar	36.29 lb/ft³ (580 kg/m³)	2	conifer	Elastic, fine-grained. Color: white - pale tan. Aromatic.	Cabinetwork, sculptire.
Black poplar	26.91 lb/ft³ (430 kg/m³)	4	hard	Color: pale red. Not resistant to changes in humidity.	Carpentry, parquet, planks, boxes, crates.
Ebony	69.45 lb/ft³ (1110 kg/m³)	1	exotic	Color: black.	Cabinetwork, sculpture, decoration. (small items).

Wood	Density	Level of hardness	Type	Characteristics	Applications
Beech	45.1 lb/ft³ (720 kg/m³)	5	hard	Color: white - pale tan. Prone to warping, cracking and rotting	Impregnated for cabinetwork.
Wallnut	41.92 lb/ft³ (670 kg/m³)	3	hard	Easy to work with. Color: grey - pale tan.	Cabinetwork and joinery.
Elm	35 lb/ft³ (560 kg/m³)	4	hard	Resilient and hard. Color: reddish.	Cabinetwork.
Black pine	31.91 lb/ft³ (510 kg/m³)	4	conifer	Color: white - pale tan - red.	Beams, trusses, stringers, hydraulic works.
Loblolly pine	31.91 lb/ft³ (510 kg/m³)	3	conifer	Color: tan. Resistant to wear.	Trusses, posts, stairways, floorboards.

Wood	Density	Level of hardness	Type	Characteristics	Applications
White oak	43.17 lb/ft^3 (690 kg/m^3)	2	hard	Color: white - red.	Carpentry, naval and hydraulic work.
Lime tree	35 lb/ft^3 (560 kg/m^3)	5	soft	Color: pale tan.	Carpentry, parquet, floor boards, crates.

Approximate holding capacity of the tools used on the worksite to mix mortar

tool	dimensions	capacity (liters)		cement (lb)	
		flush	topped up	flush	topped up
round spade	11.42inch x 1ft (29 x 32 cm)		5		16.57 (7,5 kg)
square spade	11.81inch x 1ft 1inch (30 x 34 cm)		7		22.76 (10.3 kg)
mortar carrier	1ft (33cm) diameter 6.3 inch (16cm) high	9	11	14	37.57 (17 kg)
ordinary bucket	11.81inch (30cm) diameter 9.06inch (23cm) high	11	13	17	44.2 (20 kg)
carrier basket	1ft 3.72inch (40cm) diameter 8.66inch (22cm) high	15	20	22	66.3 (30 kg)
cement bag	2ft 4.32inch x 1ft 3.72inch x 4.72inch (72 x 40 x 12 cm)		33		110.5 (50 kg)
wheelbarrow	2ft 9.48inch x 2ft 1.56inch x 5.91inch (85 x 65 x 15 cm)	60	90	70	298.35 (135 kg)
cement-mixer	large (3cv) medium (2,5 cv) small (1 cv)		300 250 100	7 - 8 m^3 / hour 5 - 6 m^3 / hour 3 - 4 m^3 / hour	
tip-bucket	large medium small	200 150 100			

gravel - lime mortar

Aggregates classified by size

Denomination	Diameter
Block	> 1ft 7.68inch *(500mm)*
Boulder	5.91inch - 1ft 7.68inch *(150 - 500mm)*
Stone	1.97inch - 5.91inch *(50 - 150mm)*
Broken stone	0.79inch - 1.97inch *(20 - 50mm)*
Coarse aggregate	0.47inch - 0.79inch *(12 - 20mm)*
Gravel	0.2inch - 0.47inch *(5 - 12mm)*
Fine aggregate	< 0.2inch *(5mm)*
Medium sand	< 0.08inch *(2mm)*
Fine sand	< 0.02inch *(0,5mm)*
Mud	0.003inch - 0.00002inch *(0,08 - 0,005mm)*
Clay	< 0.00002inch *(0,005mm)*
Colloids	< 0.00004inch *(0,001mm)*

Lime mortars and their use

The diagram below gives the mix design in related volumes of lime and sand for different uses. The quantities of water are not given as they depend on fluidity and other conditions at the worksite.

Slaked lime	1 : 1	Finish coat on walls and ceilings
	1 : 2	Rendering and thin walls
	1 : 3	Masonry walls
	1 : 4	Foundations and stone masonry
Hydraulic lime	1 : 2	Rendering and waterproof mortars
	1 : 3	Rendering y grouting
	1 : 4	Ashlar masonry

Components per m³ of hydraulic lime mortars

Mix design, batching	Lime (liters)	Sand (m³)	Water (liters)
1 : 1	251	1,255	301
1 : 2	306	1,224	306
1 : 3	387	1,161	310
1 : 4	540	1,080	324
1 : 5	874	0,847	339

Aggregates classified by size

Denomination	Diameter
Block	> 1ft 7.68inch *(500mm)*
Boulder	5.91inch - 1ft 7.68inch *(150 - 500mm)*
Stone	1.97inch - 5.91inch *(50 - 150mm)*
Broken stone	0.79inch - 1.97inch *(20 - 50mm)*
Coarse aggregate	0.47inch - 0.79inch *(12 - 20mm)*
Gravel	0.2inch - 0.47inch *(5 - 12mm)*
Fine aggregate	< 0.2inch *(5mm)*
Medium sand	< 0.08inch *(2mm)*
Fine sand	< 0.02inch *(0,5mm)*
Mud	0.003inch - 0.00002inch *(0,08 - 0,005mm)*
Clay	< 0.00002inch *(0,005mm)*
Colloids	< 0.00004inch *(0,001mm)*

Lime mortars and their use

The diagram below gives the mix design in related volumes of lime and sand for different uses. The quantities of water are not given as they depend on fluidity and other conditions at the worksite.

Slaked lime	1 : 1	Finish coat on walls and ceilings
	1 : 2	Rendering and thin walls
	1 : 3	Masonry walls
	1 : 4	Foundations and stone masonry
Hydraulic lime	1 : 2	Rendering and waterproof mortars
	1 : 3	Rendering y grouting
	1 : 4	Ashlar masonry

Components per ft³ of hydraulic lime mortars

Mix design, batching	Lime (inch³)	Sand (ft³)	Water (inch³)
1 : 1	15318.53	44.33	18370.03
1 : 2	18675.18	43.23	18675.18
1 : 3	23618.61	41	18919.3
1 : 4	32956.2	38.18	19773.72
1 : 5	53340.22	29.92	20689.17

Cement mortars

Mix design according to richness in cement (kg/m³)	Proportion in volume		Material per bag of cement (50 kilos)			Used for:
	cement	sand	sand measured in: topped up baskets	sand measured in: flush-filled wheelbarrows	mortar obtained (m³)	
600	1	2	5	1	0,083	finish coats, rendering, priming, moldings.
450	1	3	7,5	1,5	0,112	Coarse stuff, parge coats, pavements
380	1	4	10	2,5	0,132	Vaults, facing walls, stairways
300	1	5	12,5	2,5	0,166	Heavy load bearing masonry, parging
250	1	6	15	3,5	0,200	Load bearing masonry
200	1	8	20	4,5	0,250	Non-load-bearing masonry
170	1	10	25	3,5	0,333	Fillings, mortar beds

Cement mortars

Mix design according to richness in cement (lb/ft³)	Proportion in volume		Material per bag of cement (110.231 lb)			Used for:
	cement	sand	sand measured in: topped up baskets	flush-filled wheelbarrows	mortar obtained (ft³)	
37.54	1	2	5	1	2.93	finish coats, rendering, priming, moldings.
28.16	1	3	7,5	1,5	3.95	Coarse stuff, parge coats, pavements
23.78	1	4	10	2,5	4.66	Vaults, facing walls, stairways
18.77	1	5	12,5	2,5	5.86	Heavy load bearing masonry, parging
15.64	1	6	15	3,5	7.05	Load bearing masonry
12.51	1	8	20	4,5	8.83	Non-load-bearing masonry
10.64	1	10	25	3,5	11.76	Fillings, mortar beds

Concrete batching or mix design

Richness in cement (kg/m³)	Proportions			Liters			Uses
	cement	sand	gravel	cement	sand	gravel	
100	1	6	12	75	450	900	Fills, joints, hiegenic concrete
150	1	4	8	110	440	880	Trenches, foundations, unusually thick casts.
200	1	3	6	145	435	870	Retaining walls, foundation wells, slabs.
250	1	2,5	5	170	425	850	Pillars, supports, pavements
300	1	2	4	207	415	830	Reinforced concrete, footing, special walls.
350	1	2	3	240	480	720	Structural concrete, pillars, beams
400	1	1,5	3	263	395	790	Thin reinforced slabs, stress pieces, joists.
450	1	1,5	2,5	290	435	725	Special prefabricated items,pretensed items.
500	1	1	2	360	360	730	Highly specialized maximum control tasks.

Approx. water needed for 1m³: 150 - 250 liters.
Approx. weight of 1m³: 2.200 - 2.500 kg.
Weight of 1 bag of cement: - 50 kg
Volume of 1 bag of cement: - 33 liters

Concrete batching or mix design

Richness in cement (lb/ft³)	Proportions			ft³			Uses
	cement	sand	gravel	cement	sand	gravel	
6.26	1	6	12	2.65	15.89	31.78	Fills, joints, hiegenic concrete
9.39	1	4	8	3.88	15.54	31.07	Trenches, foundations, unusually thick casts.
12.51	1	3	6	5.12	15.36	30.72	Retaining walls, foundation wells, slabs.
15.64	1	2,5	5	6	15	30.01	Pillars, supports, pavements
18.77	1	2	4	7.31	14.65	29.31	Reinforced concrete, footing, special walls.
21.9	1	2	3	8.47	16.95	25.42	Structural concrete, pillars, beams
25	1	1,5	3	9.29	13.95	27.89	Thin reinforced slabs, stress pieces, joists.
28.16	1	1,5	2,5	10.24	15.36	25.6	Special prefabricated items, pretensed items.
31.29	1	1	2	12.7116	12.71	25.78	Highly specialized maximum control tasks.

Approx. water needed for 35.31ft³: 150 - 250 liters.

Approx. weight of 35.31ft³: 4850.17 - 5511.5 lb.

Weight of 1 bag of cement: - 110.231 lb

Volume of 1 bag of cement: - 33 liters

Denomination and uses of the various portland cements

Denomination	Classification		Uses
	type	class	
portland cement	I	I - 0 I	Prefabricated items and heavy duty concrete (special public works).
composite portland cement slag concrete pozzolanic portland cement portland cement with ash	II	II II - S II - Z II - C	General use concrete and mortar.
blast furnace cement	III	III - 1 III - 2	Special types of concrete for aggressive environments.
pozzolanic cement	IV	IV	Concrete and mortar for moderate environments. Hydraulic works.
mixed cement	V	V	Stabilizations, bases for roads.
aluminous cement	VI	VI	Fire-resistant or refractory concrete. For use in aggressive environments.

Common nail sizes

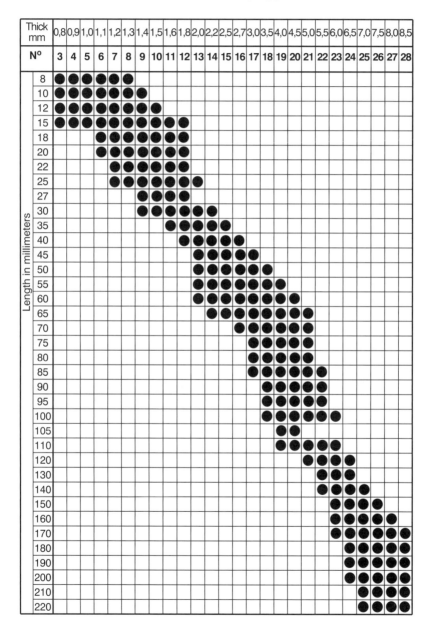

Characteristics of normal S-shape angle irons

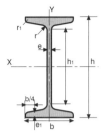

Nº	Dimensiones						Cross section terms				
	h ft	b ft	e = r ft	e1 ft	r1 ft	h1 ft	A inch²	Wx inch³	Wy inch³	iy inch	p weight lb/ft
8	3"	2"	0.5"	0.23"	0.09"	2"	1,14	1,17	0,18	0,36	438
10	4"	2"	0.27"	0.27"	0.11"	3"	1,59	2,05	0,29	0,43	612,7
12	5"	2"	0.3"	0.3"	0.12"	4"	2,13	3,28	0,44	0,49	825
14	6"	3"	0.35"	0.35"	0.13"	4"	2,75	4,91	0,64	0,56	1060,7
16	6"	3"	0.37"	0.37"	0.15"	5"	3,42	7,02	0,89	0,62	1318,3
18	7"	3"	0.41"	0.41"	0.16"	6"	4,19	9,66	1,19	0,68	1613
20	8"	4"	0.4"	0.4"	0.18"	6"	5,03	12,84	1,56	0,75	1937,3
22	9"	4"	0.48"	0.48"	0.19"	7"	5,94	16,68	1,99	0,81	2291
24	9"	4"	0.52"	0.52"	0.2"	7"	6,92	21,24	2,5	0,88	2666,7
26	10"	4"	0.56"	0.56"	0.22"	8"	8,01	26,52	3,06	0,93	3086,3
28	11"	5"	0.6"	0.6"	0.24"	9"	9,17	32,52	3,67	0,98	3536
30	12"	5"	0.64"	0.64"	0.26"	9"	10,37	39,18	4,33	1,02	3992,7
32	1'	5"	0.68"	0.68"	0.27"	10"	11,67	46,92	5,08	1,07	4501
34	1' 1"	5"	0.72"	0.72"	0.29"	11"	13,02	55,38	5,9	1,12	5016,7
36	1' 2"	6"	0.77"	0.77"	0.31"	11"	14,57	65,4	6,84	1,16	5613,3
38	1' 3"	6"	0.81"	0.81"	0.32"	1'	16,05	75,6	7,86	1,21	6188
40	1' 4"	6"	0.85"	0.85"	0.34"	1' 1"	17,7	87,6	8,94	1,25	6821,3
45	1' 6"	7"	0.96"	0.96"	0.38"	1' 2"	22,05	122,4	12,18	1,37	8471,7
50	1' 8"	7"	1"	1"	0.43"	1' 4"	27	165	16,08	1,49	10387

A. Cross sectional surface area.
Wx. Elastic bending ratio in reference to the X axis.
Wy. Elastic bending ratio in reference to the Y axis.
iy. Gyration radius on the Y axis.

Characteristics of normal S-shape angle irons

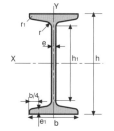

N°	Dimensiones						Cross section terms				
	h mm	b mm	e = r mm	e₁ mm	r₁ mm	h₁ mm	A cm²	Wx cm³	Wy cm³	iy mm	p weight kg/m
8	80	42	3,9	5,9	2,3	60	7,58	19,5	3	9,1	5,95
10	100	50	6,8	6,8	2,7	75	10,6	34,2	4,88	10,7	8,32
12	120	58	7,7	7,7	3,1	90	14,2	54,7	7,41	12,3	11,2
14	140	66	8,8	8,8	3,4	109	18,3	81,9	10,7	14	14,4
16	160	74	9,5	9,5	3,8	125	22,8	117	14,8	15,5	17,9
18	180	82	10,4	10,4	4,1	142	27,9	161	19,8	17,1	21,9
20	200	90	11,3	11,3	4,5	159	33,5	214	26	18,7	26,3
22	220	98	12,2	12,2	4,9	175	39,6	278	33,1	20,2	31,1
24	240	106	13,1	13,1	5,2	190	46,1	354	41,7	22	36,2
26	260	113	14,1	14,1	5,6	208	53,4	442	51	23,2	41,9
28	280	119	15,2	15,2	6,1	225	61,1	542	61,2	24,5	48
30	300	125	16,2	16,2	6,5	240	69,1	653	72,2	25,6	54,2
32	320	131	17,3	17,3	6,9	257	77,8	782	84,7	26,7	61,1
34	340	137	18,3	18,3	7,3	274	86,8	923	98,4	28	68,1
36	360	143	19,5	19,5	7,8	290	97,1	1090	114	29	76,2
38	380	149	20,5	20,5	8,2	306	107	1260	131	30,2	84
40	400	155	21,6	21,6	8,6	323	118	1460	149	31,3	92,6
45	450	170	24,3	24,3	9,7	363	147	2040	203	34,3	115
50	500	185	27	27	10,8	404	180	2750	268	37,2	141

A. Cross sectional surface area.
Wx. Elastic bending ratio in reference to the X axis.
Wy. Elastic bending ratio in reference to the Y axis.
iy. Gyration radius on the Y axis.

Characteristics of special S-shape angle irons

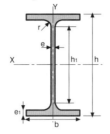

Nº	Dimensions						Cross section terms				
	h ft	b ft	e ft	e1 ft	r ft	h1 ft	A inch²	Wx inch³	Wy inch³	iy inch	p weight lb/ft
8	3.15"	1.81"	0.15"	0.2"	0.2"	2.36"	1.15	1.2	0.22	0.42	442
10	3.94"	2.17"	0.16"	0.22"	0.28"	2.95"	1.55	2.05	0.35	0.5	596.7
12	4.72"	2.52"	0.17"	0.27"	0.28"	3.66"	1.98	3.18	0.52	0.58	766
14	5.51"	2.87"	0.19"	0.25"	0.28"	4.41"	2.46	4.64	0.74	0.66	950
16	6.3"	3.23"	0.2"	0.29"	0.35"	5"	3.02	6.54	1	0.74	1163.7
18	7.09"	3.58"	0.21"	0.31"	0.35"	5.75"	3.59	8.76	1.33	0.82	1384.7
20	7.88"	3.94"	0.22"	0.33"	0.47"	6.26"	4.28	11.64	1.71	0.9	1650
22	8.66"	4.33"	0.23"	0.36"	0.47"	7"	5.01	15.12	2.24	0.99	1930
24	9.45"	4.72"	0.24"	0.39"	0.59"	7.48"	5.87	19.44	2.84	1.08	2261.3
27	10.63"	5.31"	0.26"	0.4"	0.59"	8.66"	6.89	25.74	3.73	1.21	2696
30	11.81"	5.91"	0.28"	0.42"	0.59"	9.8"	8.07	33.42	4.83	1.34	898.7
33	1'	6.3"	0.3"	0.45"	0.71"	10.67"	9.39	42.78	5.91	1.42	3617
36	1' 2"	6.69"	0.31"	0.5"	0.71"	11.77"	10.91	54.24	7.38	1.52	4206.3
40	1' 4"	7.09"	0.34"	0.53"	0.83"	13.03"	12.68	69.6	8.76	1.58	4884
45	1' 6"	4.48"	0.37"	0.57"	0.83"	1' 3"	14.83	90	1.56	1.65	5716.3
50	1' 8"	7.87"	0.4"	0.63"	0.83"	1' 5"	17.4	115.8	12.84	1.72	6681.3
55	1' 10"	8.27"	0.44"	0.68"	0.94"	1' 6"	20.1	146.4	15.24	1.78	7808.7
60	1' 12"	8.66"	0.47"	0.75"	0.94"	1' 8"	23.4	184.2	18.48	1.86	8987.3

A. Cross sectional surface area.
Wx. Elastic bending ratio in reference to the X axis.
Wy. Elastic bending ratio in reference to the Y axis.
iy. Gyration radius on the Y axis.

Characteristics of special S-shape angle irons

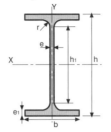

METRIC
SYSTEM

N⁰	Dimensions						Cross section terms				
	h mm	b mm	e mm	e₁ mm	r mm	h₁ mm	A cm²	Wx cm³	Wy cm³	iy mm	p weight kg/m
8	80	46	3,8	5,2	5	60	7,64	20	3,69	10,5	6
10	100	55	4,1	5,7	7	75	10,3	34,2	5,79	12,4	8,1
12	120	64	4,4	6,3	7	93	13,2	53	8,65	14,5	10,4
14	140	73	4,7	6,9	7	112	16,4	77,3	12,3	16,5	12,9
16	160	82	5	7,4	9	127	20,1	109	16,7	18,4	15,8
18	180	91	5,3	8	9	146	23,9	146	22,2	20,5	18,8
20	200	100	5,6	8,5	12	159	28,5	194	28,5	22,4	22,4
22	220	110	5,9	9,2	12	178	33,4	252	37,3	24,8	26,2
24	240	120	6,2	9,8	15	190	39,1	324	47,3	26,9	30,7
27	270	135	6,6	10,2	15	220	45,9	429	62,2	30,2	36,6
30	300	150	7,1	10,7	15	249	53,8	557	80,5	33,5	42,2
33	330	160	7,5	11,5	18	271	62,6	713	98,5	35,5	49,1
36	360	170	8	12,7	18	299	72,7	904	123	37,9	57,1
40	400	180	8,6	13,5	21	331	84,5	1160	146	39,5	66,3
45	450	190	9,4	14,6	21	379	98,8	1500	176	41,2	77,6
50	500	200	10,2	16	21	426	116	1930	214	43,1	90,7
55	550	210	11,1	17,2	24	468	134	2440	254	44,5	106
60	600	220	12	19	24	514	156	3070	308	46,6	122

A. Cross sectional surface area.
Wx. Elastic bending ratio in reference to the X axis.
Wy. Elastic bending ratio in reference to the Y axis.
iy. Gyration radius on the Y axis.

Characteristics of equal leg angle irons

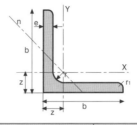

Nº	Dimensions					Cross section terms				
	b inch	e inch	r inch	r₁ inch	z inch	A inch²	Wx inch³	ix inch	Wn inch³	p weight lb/ft
20/20	**0.79**	0.12	0.14	0.08	0.24	0.17	0.02	0.24	0.01	64.7
25/25	**0.98**	0.12	0.14	0.08	0.29	0.21	0.03	0.3	0.02	82.3
30/30	**1.18**	0.12	0.2	0.1	0.33	0.26	0.04	0.36	0.03	100
40/40	**1.57**	0.16	0.24	0.12	0.44	0.46	0.09	0.48	0.07	178
40/40	**1.57**	0.24	0.24	0.12	0.47	0.67	0.14	0.48	0.09	259
45/45	**1.77**	0.2	0.28	0.14	0.5	0.65	0.15	0.54	0.11	248.7
50/50	**1.97**	0.2	0.28	0.14	0.55	0.72	0.18	0.6	0.14	277.7
50/50	**1.97**	0.24	0.28	0.14	0.59	0.98	0.25	0.6	0.17	379.3
55/55	**2.17**	0.24	0.31	0.16	0.61	0.95	0.26	0.66	0.2	364.3
60/60	**2.36**	0.28	0.31	0.16	0.67	1.04	0.32	0.73	0.24	399
60/60	**2.36**	0.31	0.31	0.16	0.7	1.35	0.41	0.72	0.29	522
65/65	**2.56**	0.28	0.35	0.18	0.73	1.31	0.43	0.78	0.32	503
70/70	**2.76**	0.28	0.35	0.18	0.78	1.41	0.51	0.85	0.38	543.3
70/70	**2.76**	0.35	0.35	0.18	0.81	1.79	0.64	0.84	0.46	688
75/75	**2.95**	0.31	0.39	0.2	0.84	1.73	0.66	0.9	0.49	665
80/80	**3.15**	0.31	0.39	0.2	0.89	1.85	0.76	0.97	0.56	711.3
80/80	**3.15**	0.39	0.39	0.2	0.92	2.27	0.93	0.96	0.65	876.3
90/90	**3.54**	0.35	0.43	0.22	1	2.33	1.08	1.1	0.8	898.7
90/90	**3.54**	0.43	0.43	0.22	1.03	2.81	1.3	1.09	0.92	1082.7
100/100	**3.94**	0.39	0.47	0.24	1.11	2.88	1.48	1.22	1.1	1112.3
100/100	**3.94**	0.47	0.47	0.24	1.14	3.41	1.75	1.21	1.26	1311
120/120	**4.72**	0.43	0.51	0.26	1.32	3.81	2.37	1.46	1.77	1465.7
120/120	**4.72**	0.51	0.51	0.26	1.35	4.46	2.76	1.46	2	1716.3
130/130	**5.12**	0.47	0.55	0.28	1.43	4.5	3.02	1.59	2.26	1738.3
130/130	**5.12**	0.55	0.55	0.28	1.46	5.21	3.49	1.58	2.54	2003.7
150/150	**5.91**	0.55	0.63	0.31	1.66	6.05	4.69	1.83	3.5	2327.7

A. Cross sectional surface area.
Wx. Elastic bending ratio in reference to the X axis.
Wy. Elastic bending ratio in reference to the Y axis.
ix. Gyration radius on the X axis.

Characteristics of equal leg angle irons

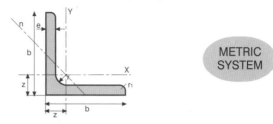

METRIC SYSTEM

Nº	Dimensions					Cross section terms				
	b mm	e mm	r mm	r₁ mm	z mm	A cm²	Wx cm³	ix mm	Wn cm³	p weight kg/m
20/20	20	3	3,5	2	6	1,12	0,28	5,9	0,18	0,88
25/25	25	3	3,5	2	7,3	1,42	0,45	7,5	0,30	1,12
30/30	30	3	5	2,5	8,4	1,74	0,65	9	0,48	1,36
40/40	40	4	6	3	11,2	3,08	1,56	12,1	1,18	2,42
40/40	40	6	6	3	12	4,48	2,26	11,9	1,57	3,52
45/45	45	5	7	3,5	12,8	4,30	2,43	13,5	1,80	3,38
50/50	50	5	7	3,5	14	4,80	3,05	15,1	2,32	3,77
50/50	50	7	7	3,5	14,9	6,56	4,15	14,9	2,85	5,15
55/55	55	6	8	4	15,6	6,31	4,40	16,6	3,28	4,95
60/60	60	6	8	4	16,9	6,91	5,29	18,2	3,95	5,42
60/60	60	8	8	4	17,7	9,03	6,88	18	4,84	7,09
65/65	65	7	9	4,5	18,5	8,70	7,18	19,6	5,27	6,83
70/70	70	7	9	4,5	19,7	9,40	8,43	21,2	6,31	7,38
70/70	70	9	9	4,5	20,5	11,9	10,6	21	7,59	9,34
75/75	75	8	10	5	21,3	11,5	11	22,6	8,11	9,03
80/80	80	8	10	5	22,6	12,3	12,6	24,2	9,25	9,66
80/80	80	10	10	5	23,4	15,1	15,5	24,1	10,9	11,9
90/90	90	9	11	5,5	25,4	15,5	18	27,4	13,3	12,2
90/90	90	11	11	5,5	26,2	18,7	21,6	27,2	15,4	14,7
100/100	100	10	12	6	28,2	19,2	24,7	30,4	18,4	15,1
100/100	100	12	12	6	29	22,7	29,2	30,2	21	17,8
120/120	120	11	13	6,5	33,6	25,4	39,5	36,6	29,5	19,9
120/120	120	13	13	6,5	34,4	29,7	46	36,4	33,3	23,3
130/130	130	12	14	7	36,4	30	50,4	39,7	37,7	23,6
130/130	130	14	14	7	37,2	34,7	58,2	39,4	42,4	27,2
150/150	150	14	16	8	42,1	40,3	78,2	45,8	58,3	31,6

A. Cross sectional surface area.
Wx. Elastic bending ratio in reference to the X axis.
Wy. Elastic bending ratio in reference to the Y axis.
ix. Gyration radius on the X axis.

steel angle irons

Characteristics of unequal leg angle irons

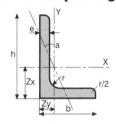

IMPERIAL SYSTEM

N⁰	Dimensions						Cross section terms				
	h inch	b inch	e=r inch	Zx inch	Zy inch	a graus	A inch²	ix inch	Wy inch³	Wx inch³	p weight lb/ft
30/20	**1.19**	**0.79**	0.16	0.38	1.99	23,4	0.28	0.48	0.05	0.1	109.03
40/25	**1.57**	**0.98**	0.18	0.54	0.22	20,46	0.41	0.5	0.04	0.1	158.38
50/30	**1.97**	**1.18**	0.2	0.68	0.26	19,15	0.57	0.63	0.07	0.17	218.05
60/40	**2.36**	**1.57**	0.2	0.77	0.29	23,40	0.72	0.76	0.12	0.26	276.25
70/50	**2.76**	**1.97**	0.24	0.88	0.39	26,33	1.03	0.88	0.23	0.42	397.8
70/50	**2.76**	**1.97**	0.28	0.89	0.49	26,23	1.19	0.88	0.26	0.48	460.42
80/50	**3.15**	**1.97**	0.24	1.05	0.51	21,19	1.12	1.02	0.23	0.55	432.42
80/50	**3.15**	**1.97**	0.31	1.07	0.46	20,58	1.47	1.01	0.3	0.71	568.71
90/60	**3.54**	**2.36**	0.2	1.13	0.49	24	1.09	1.16	0.29	0.6	420.64
90/60	**3.54**	**2.36**	0.28	1.15	0.57	23,43	1.5	1.14	0.39	0.82	581.97
90/60	**3.54**	**2.36**	0.35	1.18	0.6	23,28	1.92	1.13	0.48	1.02	736.67
90/75	**3.54**	**2.95**	0.35	1.08	0.79	34,11	2.12	1.12	0.76	1.06	817.7
90/75	**3.54**	**2.95**	0.43	1.11	0.82	34,02	2.57	1.1	0.9	1.26	987.13
100/70	**3.94**	**2.76**	0.39	1.29	0.7	25,31	2.42	1.25	0.73	1.41	928.2
100/70	**3.94**	**2.76**	0.47	1.31	0.73	25,17	2.87	1.24	0.85	1.66	1105
100/85	**3.94**	**3.35**	0.39	1.19	0.9	35,18	2.64	1.24	1.08	1.45	1016.6
100/85	**3.94**	**3.35**	0.47	1.22	0.93	35,09	3.14	1.22	1.26	1.7	1208.13
110/70	**4.33**	**2.76**	0.31	1.43	0.65	22	2.07	1.4	0.61	1.39	802.97
110/90	**4.33**	**3.54**	0.39	1.32	0.93	33,20	2.87	1.37	1.23	1.76	1105
110/90	**4.33**	**3.54**	0.47	1.35	0.96	33,07	3.41	1.36	1.43	2.08	1311.27
120/80	**4.72**	**3.15**	0.39	1.55	0.77	23,40	2.87	1.52	0.98	2.05	1105
120/80	**4.72**	**3.15**	0.47	1.57	0.8	23,28	3.41	1.51	1.15	2.42	1311.27
125/100	**4.92**	**3.94**	0.43	1.51	1.02	32,03	3.56	1.56	1.67	2.51	1370.2
125/100	**4.92**	**3.94**	0.51	1.54	1.05	32,21	4.16	1.54	1.93	2.87	1605.93
150/75	**5.91**	**2.95**	0.39	2.1	0.64	14,47	3.24	1.93	0.88	3.11	1252.3

A. Cross sectional surface area.
Wx. Elastic bending ratio in reference to the X axis.
Wy. Elastic bending ratio in reference to the Y axis.
ix. Gyration radius on the X axis.

Characteristics of unequal leg angle irons

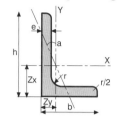

METRIC
SYSTEM

N°	Dimensions						Cross section terms				
	h mm	b mm	e=r mm	Zx mm	Zy mm	a graus	A cm²	ix mm	Wy cm³	Wx cm³	p weight kg/m
30/20	30	20	4	9,7	5,6	23,4	1,88	12	0,76	1,62	1,48
40/25	40	25	4,5	13,8	6,5	20,46	2,74	12,5	0,68	1,64	2,15
50/30	50	30	5	17,3	7,4	19,15	3,78	15,7	1,11	2,86	2,96
60/40	60	40	5	19,6	9,8	23,40	4,78	19	2,04	4,28	3,75
70/50	70	50	6	22,4	12,5	26,33	6,88	22,1	3,81	7,04	5,40
70/50	70	50	7	22,7	12,9	26,23	7,96	21,9	4,35	8,08	6,25
80/50	80	50	6	26,6	11,7	21,19	7,48	25,5	3,86	9,11	5,87
80/50	80	50	8	27,2	12,5	20,58	9,83	25,2	4,95	11,8	7,72
90/60	90	60	5	28,6	13,8	24	7,28	28,9	4,79	9,94	5,71
90/60	90	60	7	29,3	14,5	23,43	10,01	28,6	6,47	13,6	7,90
90/60	90	60	9	30	15,2	23,28	12,8	28,3	8,04	17	10
90/75	90	75	9	27,5	20,1	34,11	14,1	27,9	12,6	17,6	11,1
90/75	90	75	11	28,2	20,8	34,02	17,1	27,6	15	21	13,4
100/70	100	70	10	32,7	17,9	25,31	16,1	31,3	12,2	23,5	12,6
100/70	100	70	12	33,4	18,6	25,17	19,1	31	14,2	27,6	15
100/85	100	85	10	30,3	22,9	35,18	17,6	31	18	24,2	13,8
100/85	100	85	12	31	23,6	35,09	20,9	30,6	21	28,4	16,4
110/70	110	70	8	36,2	16,4	22	13,8	35,1	10,1	23,1	10,9
110/90	110	90	10	33,6	23,7	33,20	19,1	34,3	20,5	29,4	15
110/90	110	90	12	34,2	24,4	33,07	22,7	34	23,9	34,6	17,8
120/80	120	80	10	39,3	19,5	23,40	19,1	38	16,3	34,2	15
120/80	120	80	12	39,9	20,2	23,28	22,7	37,7	19,1	40,3	17,8
125/100	125	100	11	38,4	26	32,03	23,7	39,1	27,8	41,8	18,6
125/100	125	100	13	39	26,7	32,21	27,7	38,5	32,2	47,8	21,8
150/75	15	75	10	53,3	16,2	14,47	21,6	48,2	14,6	51,9	17

A. Cross sectional surface area.
Wx. Elastic bending ratio in reference to the X axis.
Wy. Elastic bending ratio in reference to the Y axis.
ix. Gyration radius on the X axis.

steel angle irons

Characteristics of standard channel angle irons

 IMPERIAL SYSTEM

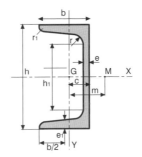

Nº	Dimensions						Cross section terms						
	h inch	b inch	e inch	e₁=r inch	r₁ inch	h₁ inch	A inch²	Wx inch³	Wy inch³	iy inch	c inch	m inch	p weight lb/ft
8	**3.15**	**1.77**	0.24	0.31	0.16	1.81	1.65	1.59	0.38	0.53	0.58	1.07	636.48
10	**3.94**	**1.97**	0.24	0.33	0.18	2.52	2.03	2.47	0.51	0.59	0.62	1.17	780.87
12	**4.72**	**2.17**	0.28	0.35	0.18	3.23	2.55	3.64	0.67	0.64	0.64	1.21	987.13
14	**5.51**	**2.37**	0.28	0.39	0.2	3.86	3.06	5.18	0.89	0.7	0.7	1.35	1178.67
16	**6.3**	**2.56**	0.3	0.41	0.22	4.53	3.6	6.96	1.1	0.76	0.74	1.42	1384.93
18	**7.09**	**2.76**	0.31	0.43	0.22	5.24	4.2	9	1.34	0.81	0.77	1.5	1620.67
20	**7.87**	**2.95**	0.33	0.45	0.24	5.94	4.83	11.46	1.62	0.86	0.8	1.58	1863.77
22	**8.66**	**3.15**	0.35	0.49	0.26	6.57	5.61	14.7	2.01	0.92	0.86	1.68	2165.8
25/8	**9.84**	**3.15**	0.39	0.49	0.26	7.76	6.35	17.94	2.05	0.88	0.79	1.5	2445.73
25/10	**9.84**	**3.94**	0.39	0.63	0.31	7.17	8.06	25.02	3.94	1.18	1.16	2.31	3108.73
30	**11.81**	**3.54**	0.51	0.55	0.16	9.49	9.06	29.1	2.98	0.95	0.84	1.5	3491.8

A. Cross sectional surface area.
Wx. Elastic bending ratio in reference to the X axis.
Wy. Elastic bending ratio in reference to the Y axis.
iy. Gyration radius on the Y axis.

Characteristics of standard channel angle irons

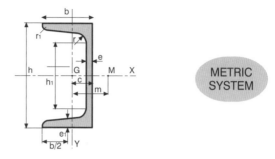

METRIC
SYSTEM

Nº	Dimensions						Cross section terms						
	h mm	b mm	e mm	e₁=r mm	r₁ mm	h₁ mm	A cm²	Wx cm³	Wy cm³	iy mm	c mm	m mm	p weight kg/m
8	80	45	6	8	4	46	11	26,5	6,36	13,3	14,5	26,7	8,64
10	100	50	6	8,5	4,5	64	13,5	41,2	8,49	14,7	15,5	29,3	10,6
12	120	55	7	9	4,5	82	17	60,7	11,1	15,9	16	30,3	13,4
14	140	60	7	10	5	98	20,4	86,4	14,8	17,5	17,5	33,7	16
16	160	65	7,5	10,5	5,5	115	24	116	18,3	18,9	18,4	35,6	18,8
18	180	70	8	11	5,5	133	28	150	22,4	20,2	19,2	37,5	22
20	200	75	8,5	11,5	6	151	32,2	191	27	21,4	20,1	39,4	25,3
22	220	80	9	12,5	6,5	167	37,4	245	33,6	23	21,4	42	29,4
25/8	250	80	10	12,5	6,5	197	42,3	299	34,1	22	19,7	37,6	33,2
25/10	250	100	10	16	8	182	53,7	417	65,6	29,4	29	57,7	42,2
30	300	90	13	14	4	241	60,4	485	49,7	23,8	20,9	37,5	47,4

A. Cross sectional surface area.
Wx. Elastic bending ratio in reference to the X axis.
Wy. Elastic bending ratio in reference to the Y axis.
iy. Gyration radius on the Y axis.

steel angle irons

Characteristics of W-shape wide flange angle irons

IMPERIAL
SYSTEM

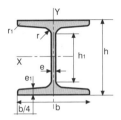

Nº	Dimensions							Cross section terms				p
	h inch	b inch	e inch	e₁ inch	r inch	r₁ inch	h₁ inch	A inch²	Wx inch³	Wy inch³	iy inch	weight lb/ft
14	**5.51**	**5.51**	0.33	0.49	0.33	0.17	3.54	6.83	13.14	4.9	1.42	2629.9
16	**6.3**	**6.3**	0.35	0.53	0.35	0.18	4.13	8.4	18.72	6.9	1.62	3241.3
18	**7.09**	**7.09**	0.37	0.57	0.37	0.19	4.72	10.13	25.68	9.36	1.82	3904.3
20	**7.87**	**7.87**	0.39	0.61	0.39	0.2	5.31	12	34.14	12.42	2.03	4626.27
22	**8.66**	**8.66**	0.41	0.65	0.41	0.21	5.91	14	44.16	15.96	2.24	5392.4

A. Cross sectional surface area.
Wx . Elastic bending ratio in reference to the X axis.
Wy. Elastic bending ratio in reference to the Y axis.
iy. Gyration radius on the Y axis.

Characteristics of W-shape wide flange angle irons

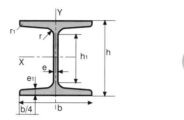

Nº	Dimensions							Cross section terms				
	h mm	b mm	e mm	e_1 mm	r mm	r_1 mm	h_1 mm	A cm²	Wx cm³	Wy cm³	iy mm	p weight kg/m
14	140	140	8,5	12,5	8,5	4,25	90	45,5	219	81,7	35,5	35,7
16	160	160	9	13,5	9	4,50	105	56	312	115	40,6	44
18	180	180	9,5	14,5	9,5	4,75	120	67,5	428	156	45,6	53
20	200	200	10	15,5	10	5	135	80	569	207	50,8	62,8
22	220	220	10,5	16,5	10,5	5,25	150	93,3	736	266	56	73,2

A. Cross sectional surface area.
Wx . Elastic bending ratio in reference to the X axis.
Wy. Elastic bending ratio in reference to the Y axis.
iy. Gyration radius on the Y axis.

Characteristics of normal structural T angle irons

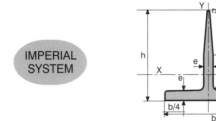

IMPERIAL
SYSTEM

Nº	Dimensions					Cross section terms					p
	h inch	b inch	e=r inch	r₁ inch	r₂ inch	A inch²	Wx inch³	Wy inch³	iy inch	z inch	weight lb/ft
30	**1.18**	**1.18**	0.16	0.08	0.04	0.34	0.05	0.03	0.25	0.34	130.39
35	**1.38**	**1.38**	0.18	0.1	0.04	0.45	0.07	0.05	0.29	0.4	171.64
40	**1.57**	**1.57**	0.2	0.1	0.04	0.57	0.11	0.08	0.33	0.45	218.05
50	**1.97**	**1.97**	0.24	0.12	0.06	0.85	0.2	0.15	0.41	0.56	327.08
60	**2.36**	**2.36**	0.28	0.14	0.08	1.19	0.33	0.24	0.5	0.66	458.94
70	**2.76**	**2.76**	0.31	0.16	0.08	1.59	0.53	0.38	0.58	0.78	612.91
80	**3.15**	**3.15**	0.35	0.18	0.08	2.04	0.77	0.56	0.66	0.89	788.23
100	**3.94**	**3.94**	0.43	0.22	0.12	3.14	1.48	1.06	0.82	1.1	1208.13

Characteristics of special structural T angle irons

IMPERIAL
SYSTEM

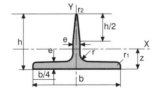

Nº	Dimensions					Cross section terms					p
	h inch	b inch	e=r inch	r₁ inch	r₂ inch	A inch²	Wx inch³	Wy inch³	iy inch	z inch	weight lb/ft
60	**2.36**	**3.94**	0.31	0.16	0.08	1.8	0.28	0.58	0.8	0.55	694.68
75	**2.95**	**3.94**	0.31	0.16	0.08	1.98	0.66	1.06	1.03	0.68	766.13

A. Cross sectional surface area.
W. Elastic bending ratio in reference to the X axis.
Wy. Elastic bending ratio in reference to the Y axis.
iy. Gyration radius on the Y axis.

Characteristics of normal structural T angle irons

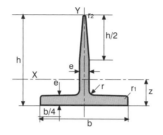

N°	Dimensions					Cross section terms					
	h mm	b mm	e=r mm	r₁ mm	r₂ mm	A cm²	Wx cm³	Wy cm³	iy mm	z mm	p weight kg/m
30	30	30	4	2	1	2,26	0,80	0,58	6,2	8,5	1,77
35	35	35	4,5	2,5	1	2,97	1,23	0,90	7,3	9,9	2,33
40	40	40	5	2,5	1	3,77	1,84	1,29	8,3	11,2	2,96
50	50	50	6	3	1,5	5,66	3,36	2,42	10,3	13,9	4,44
60	60	60	7	3,5	2	7,94	5,48	4,07	12,4	16,6	6,23
70	70	70	8	4	2	10,6	8,79	6,32	14,4	19,4	8,32
80	80	80	9	4,5	2	13,6	12,8	9,25	16,5	22,2	10,7
100	100	100	11	5,5	3	20,9	24,6	17,7	20,5	27,4	16,4

Characteristics of special structural T angle irons

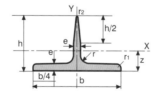

N°	Dimensions					Cross section terms					
	h mm	b mm	e=r mm	r₁ mm	r₂ mm	A cm²	Wx cm³	Wy cm³	iy mm	z mm	p weight kg/m
60	60	100	8	4	2	12	4,63	9,60	20	13,7	9,43
75	75	100	8	4	2	13,2	11	17,6	25,8	17	10,40

A. Cross sectional surface area.
W. Elastic bending ratio in reference to the X axis.
Wy. Elastic bending ratio in reference to the Y axis.
iy. Gyration radius on the Y axis.

Characteristics of rectangular structural tubing

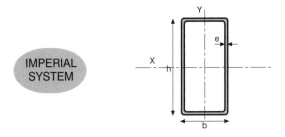

N°	Dimensions			Cross section terms		
	h inch	b inch	e inch	A inch²	Wx inch³	p weight lb/ft
30/40	**1.18**	**1.18**	0.16	0.34	0.05	130.39
35	**1.38**	**1.38**	0.18	0.45	0.07	171.64
40	**1.57**	**1.57**	0.2	0.57	0.11	218.05
50	**1.97**	**1.97**	0.24	0.85	0.2	327.08
60	**2.36**	**2.36**	0.28	1.19	0.33	458.94
70	**2.76**	**2.76**	0.31	1.59	0.53	612.91
80	**3.15**	**3.15**	0.35	2.04	0.77	788.23
100	**3.94**	**3.94**	0.43	3.14	1.48	1208.13

A. Cross sectional surface area.
Wx. Elastic bending ratio in reference to the X axis.

Characteristics of rectangular structural tubing

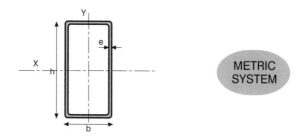

METRIC
SYSTEM

Nº	Dimensions			Cross section terms		
	h mm	b mm	e mm	A cm²	Wx cm³	p weight kg/m
30/40	30	30	4	2,26	0,80	1,77
35	35	35	4,5	2,97	1,23	2,33
40	40	40	5	3,77	1,84	2,96
50	50	50	6	5,66	3,36	4,44
60	60	60	7	7,94	5,48	6,23
70	70	70	8	10,6	8,79	8,32
80	80	80	9	13,6	12,8	10,7
100	100	100	11	20,9	24,6	16,4

A. Cross sectional surface area.
Wx. Elastic bending ratio in reference to the X axis.

Characteristics of square and round structural tubing

d

d

d inch	A section surface inch²	e inch	p weight lb/ft	d inch	A section surface inch²	circ. inch	p weight lb/ft	d inch	A section surface inch²	circ. ft	p weight lb/ft
0.31	0.1	0.45	0.34	0.2	0.03	0.62	0.1	1.38	1.44	4.33"	5.09
0.39	0.15	0.56	0.53	0.24	0.04	0.74	0.15	1.57	1.88	4.95"	6.64
0.47	0.22	0.67	0.76	0.28	0.06	0.87	0.2	1.77	2.39	5.57"	8.42
0.55	0.29	0.78	1.19	0.31	0.08	0.99	0.27	1.97	2.94	6.18"	10.38
0.63	0.38	0.89	1.35	0.35	0.1	1.11	0.34	2.17	3.56	6.8"	12.6
0.71	0.49	1	1.71	0.39	0.12	1.24	0.42	2.36	4.24	7.42"	14.96
0.79	0.6	1.11	2.12	0.47	0.17	1.48	0.6	2.56	4.98	8.04"	17.52
0.87	0.67	1.22	2.56	0.55	0.23	1.73	0.82	2.76	5.77	8.66"	20.35
0.98	0.94	1.39	3.31	0.63	0.3	1.98	1.06	3.15	7.54	9.89"	26.61
1.1	1.18	1.56	4.14	0.71	0.38	2.23	1.35	3.54	9.54	11.13"	33.62
1.18	1.35	1.67	4.76	0.79	0.47	2.47	1.66	3.94	11.78	1'	41.57
1.38	1.84	1.95	6.48	0.87	0.57	2.72	2	4.33	14.25	1' 2"	50.26
1.57	2.4	2.23	8.49	0.98	0.74	3.09	2.59	4.72	16.97	1' 3"	59.83
1.77	3.04	2.51	10.71	1.1	0.92	3.46	3.25	5.51	23.09	1' 5"	81.53
1.97	3.75	2.78	13.21	1.18	1.06	3.71	3.74	6.3	3.02	1' 8"	106.46
2.36	5.4	3.34	19.07	1.26	1.21	3.96	4.25	7.87	47.12	2'	166.42
2.76	7.35	3.9	25.94								
3.15	9.6	4.45	33.82								
3.54	12.15	5.01	42.85								
3.94	15	5.57	52.89								

Characteristics of square and round structural tubing

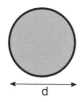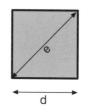

METRIC SYSTEM

d mm	A section surface cm²	e mm	p weight kg/m	d mm	A section surface cm²	circ. mm	p weight kg/m	d mm	A section surface cm²	circ. mm	p weight kg/m
8	0,64	11,31	0,50	5	0,196	15,70	0,154	35	9,621	109,9	7,55
10	1	14,14	0,78	6	0,282	18,85	0,222	40	12,56	125,7	9,86
12	1,44	16,97	1,13	7	0,384	21,99	0,302	45	15,9	141,4	12,5
14	1,96	19,80	1,77	8	0,502	25,13	0,395	50	19,63	157,1	15,4
16	2,56	22,63	2,01	9	0,636	28,27	0,499	55	23,76	172,8	18,7
18	3,24	25,45	2,54	10	0,785	31,41	0,617	60	28,27	188,5	22,2
20	4	28,28	3,14	12	1,130	37,69	0,888	65	33,18	204,2	26
22	4,84	31,10	3,80	14	1,539	43,98	1,21	70	38,48	219,9	30,2
25	6,25	35,35	4,91	16	2,01	50,26	1,58	80	50,26	251,3	39,5
28	7,84	39,60	6,15	18	2,554	56,54	2	90	63,62	282,8	49,9
30	9	42,42	7,07	20	3,141	62,83	2,47	100	78,54	314,1	61,7
35	12,25	49,50	9,62	22	3,801	69,11	2,98	110	95,03	345,6	74,6
40	16	56,57	12,6	25	4,908	78,54	3,85	120	113,1	377	88,8
45	20,25	63,64	15,9	28	6,157	87,96	4,83	140	153,9	439,8	121
50	25	70,71	19,6	30	7,068	94,28	5,55	160	201,1	502,6	158
60	36	84,85	28,3	32	8,042	100,5	6,31	200	314,1	628,3	247
70	49	98,99	38,5								
80	64	113,14	50,2								
90	81	127,28	63,6								
100	100	141,42	78,5								

aluminum angle irons

Characteristics of aluminum angle irons

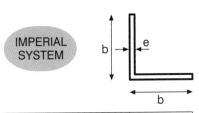

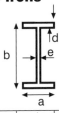

IMPERIAL SYSTEM

b inch	e inch	p weight lb/ft
1.18	0.1	0.27
1.57	0.12	0.44
1.97	0.12	0.56
1.97	0.2	1.09
2.36	0.14	0.79
3.15	0.2	1.5
3.15	0.24	1.75
3.94	0.24	2.25
3.94	0.31	2.9
4.72	0.28	3.15
4.72	0.39	4.36

b inch	a inch	e inch	d inch	p weight lb/ft
2.36	1.18	0.16	0.24	1.07
3.15	1.57	0.2	0.28	1.71
3.94	1.97	0.24	0.31	2.51
4.72	2.36	0.24	0.35	3.21
5.51	2.76	0.28	0.39	4.27
6.3	3.15	0.28	0.43	5.15

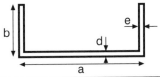

b inch	a inch	e inch	d inch	p weight lb/ft
2.36	1.18	0.2	0.24	1.14
3.15	1.38	0.2	0.28	1.54
3.94	1.57	0.24	0.31	2.16
4.72	1.97	0.24	0.35	2.82
5.51	2.36	0.28	0.39	3.81
6.3	2.76	0.28	0.39	4.43
7.09	2.95	0.31	0.43	5.43
7.87	3.15	0.31	0.47	6.19
9.45	3.94	0.35	0.51	8.42

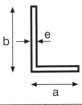

b inch	a inch	e inch	p weight lb/ft
1.97	1.5	0.12	0.5
1.97	1.5	0.16	0.64
2.36	1.77	0.14	0.69
2.36	1.77	0.2	0.95
3.15	2.36	0.2	1.32
3.15	2.36	0.24	1.52
3.94	2.95	0.24	1.98
3.94	2.95	0.31	2.54
4.72	3.54	0.28	2.77
4.72	3.54	0.39	3.81
5.51	4.13	0.33	3.93
5.51	4.13	0.43	4.89

b inch	a inch	e inch	p weight lb/ft
1.97	1.5	0.16	0.64
2.36	1.77	0.2	0.96
3.15	2.36	0.24	1.53
3.94	2.95	0.31	2.55
4.72	3.54	0.39	3.83

Characteristics of aluminum angle irons

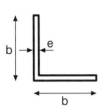

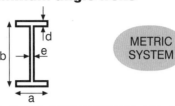

METRIC SYSTEM

b mm	e mm	p weight kg/m
30	2,5	0,404
40	3	0,647
50	3	0,836
50	5	1,62
60	3,5	1,17
80	5	2,23
80	6	2,59
100	6	3,34
100	8	4,31
120	7	4,68
120	10	6,47

b mm	a mm	e mm	d mm	p weight kg/m
60	30	4	6	1,59
80	40	5	7	2,54
100	50	6	8	3,72
120	60	6	9	4,77
140	70	7	10	6,33
160	80	7	11	7,64

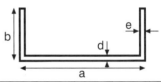

b mm	a mm	e mm	d mm	p weight kg/m
60	30	5	6	1,69
80	35	5	7	2,29
100	40	6	8	3,20
120	50	6	9	4,19
140	60	7	10	5,66
160	70	7	10	6,58
180	75	8	11	8,06
200	80	8	12	9,19
240	100	9	13	12,5

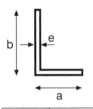

b mm	a mm	e mm	p weight kg/m
50	38	3	0,738
50	38	4	0,947
60	45	3,5	1,03
60	45	5	1,412
80	60	5	1,96
80	60	6	2,26
100	75	6	2,94
100	75	8	3,77
120	90	7	4,11
120	90	10	5,65
140	105	8,5	5,83
140	105	11	7,26

b mm	a mm	e mm	p weight kg/m
50	38	4	0,952
60	45	5	1,42
80	60	6	2,27
100	75	8	3,79
120	90	10	5,68

Standard sizes of various glass sheets

IMPERIAL SYSTEM

Denomination	Thickness inch	Tol. inch	Maximum size ft
Thin glass	0.02-0.05		1' 12"x4' 2"
	0.05-0.07		2' 7"x5' 3"
	0.07-0.08		1' 12"x6' 2"
normal glass		0.01	
EM	0.11	0.01	3' 11"x6' 2"
ED	0.15	0.01	4' 7"x7'
extra-thick glass	0.18	0.01	9'x16' 5"
	0.22	0.02	9' 10"x16' 5'
	0.26	0.03	9' 10"x16' 5'
	0.31	0.03	8' 6"x16' 6"
	0.39	0.04	8' 6"x12' 12'
	0.47	0.04	8' 6"x11' 10'
	0.59	0.04	8' 6"x9' 10"
	0.75		8' 6"x9' 10"
	0.83		8' 6"x9' 10"
Clear glass transparent		0.01	
	0.16	0.01	10' 5"x19' 8'
	0.2	0.01	10' 5"x19' 8'
	0.24	0.01	10' 5"x19' 8'
	0.31	0.01	10' 5"x24' 7'
	0.39	0.01	10' 5"x29' 6'
	0.47	0.01	10' 5"x29' 6'
	0.59	0.04	10' 5"x19' 8'
	0.75	0.04	9' 3"x14' 9"
	0.83		9' 1"x14' 9"

Denomination	Thickness inch	Tol. inch	Maximum size ft
colored glass			
bronze	0.16	0.01	10' 4"x19' 8"
gray	0.2	0.01	10' 4"x19' 8"
	0.24	0.01	10' 4"x19' 8"
	0.31	0.01	10' 4"x19' 8"
	0.39	0.01	10' 4"x19' 8"
	0.47	0.01	10' 4"x19' 8"
	0.16	0.01	10' 4"x19' 8"
green	0.24	0.01	10' 4"x19' 8"
	0.31	0.01	10' 4"x19' 8"
	0.39	0.01	10' 4"x19' 8"
	0.47	0.01	10' 4"x19' 8"
Reflecting glass silver	0.31	0.04	5' 11"x14' 6"
134	0.24	0.04	5' 10"x14' 6"
178	0.31	0.04	5' 10"x14' 6"
	0.39	0.04	5' 10"x14' 6"
	0.47	0.04	5' 10"x14' 6"
	0.24	0.02	8' 3"x14' 9"
	0.31	0.02	8' 3"x14' 9"
200	0.39	0.02	8' 3"x14' 9"
	0.47	0.02	8' 3"x14' 9"
	0.24	0.04	7' 10"x14' 7"
	0.31	0.04	7' 10"x14' 7"
274	0.39	0.04	7' 10"x14' 7"

Standard sizes of various glass sheets

Denomination	Thickness mm	Tol. mm	Maximum size mm
colored glass *bronze* *gray*	4	0,2	3150x6000
	5	0,2	3150x6000
	6	0,2	3150x6000
	8	0,3	3150x6000
	10	0,3	3150x6000
	12	0,3	3150x6000
green	4	0,2	3150x6000
	6	0,2	3150x6000
	8	0,3	3150x6000
	10	0,3	3150x6000
	12	0,3	3150x6000
Reflecting glass silver *134* *178* *200* *274*	8	1,0	1800x4410
	6	1,0	1770x4410
	8	1,0	1770x4410
	10	1,0	1770x4410
	12	1,0	1770x4410
	6	0,5	2520x4500
	8	0,5	2520x4500
	10	0,5	2520x4500
	12	0,5	2520x4500
	6	1,0	2400x4440
	8	1,0	2400x4440
	10	1,0	2400x4440

METRIC SYSTEM

Denomination	Thickness mm	Tol. mm	Maximum size mm
Thin glass	0,6-1,2		600x1260
	1,2-1,8		800x1600
	1,75-2,0		600x1880
normal glass *EM* *ED*		0,2	
	2,8	0,2	1200x1880
	3,8	0,3	1400x2160
extra-thick glass	4,5	0,3	2760x5000
	5,5	0,3	3000x5000
	6,5	0,5	3000x5000
	8	0,7	2600x5040
	10	0,8	2600x3960
	12	1,0	2600x3600
	15	1,0	2600x3000
	19	1,0	2600x3000
	21		2600x3000
Clear glass transparent		0,2	
	4	0,2	3180x6000
	5	0,2	3180x6000
	6	0,3	3180x6000
	8	0,3	3180x7500
	10	0,3	3180x9000
	12	0,3	3180x9000
	15	1,0	3180x6000
	19	1,0	2820x4500
	21		2760x4500

IMPERIAL
SYSTEM

Insulation glass, standard sizes

Type of glass	Size ft	Thickness inch	LZR ft	Surface ft²
2 x normal glass EM	2' 6"x4' 11"	0.73	0.47	12.16
2 x normal glass ED	4' 8"x7'10"	0.81	0.47	36.15
2 x thick glass 4,5 mm	5' 7"x8'10"	0.85	0.47	36.58
2 x thick glass 5,5 mm	16' 5"x8'10"	0.93	0.47	86.08
2 x thick glass 6,5 mm	16' 5"x8'10"	1	0.47	86.08
2 x thick glass 8 - 10 - 12 mm	16' 5"x8' 10"	1.12-1.44	0.47	86.08
2 x reflecting glass 5 mm	9' 10"x8'10"	0.89	0.47	64.56
2 x reflecting glass 6 mm	16' 5"x9'10"	0.96	0.47	64.56
2 x reflecting glass 8 mm	16' 5"x9'10"	1.12	0.47	96.84
2 x reflecting glass 10 + 12 mm	16' 5"x9'10"	1.28-1.44	0.47	107.6

LZR (Spacer) The space between two sheets of glass.

Glass tiles, of various types and sizes

Type	size ft	Thickness inch
Primalit *square*	7.87"x7.87"	2.36
Primalit *rectangular*	10.63"x5.91"	2.36
Baldulux *square*	7.87"x7.87"	1.32
Baldulux *rectangular*	1'x5.79"	1.32
Great Baldulux *rectangular*	1' 2"x7.48"	1.52
Gemax *square*	7.48"x7.48"	3.84
Catolux	11.81"x2.36"	1.57
Nevada *C - 32 y L - 32*	7.87"x7.87"	1.26

Insulation glass, standard sizes

Type of glass	Size cm	Thickness mm	LZR mm	Surface m²
2 x normal glass EM	75 x 150	18,5	12	1,13
2 x normal glass ED	141 x 240	20,5	12	3,36
2 x thick glass 4,5 mm	170 x 270	21,5	12	3,40
2 x thick glass 5,5 mm	500 x 270	23,5	12	8,00
2 x thick glass 6,5 mm	500 x 270	25,5	12	8,00
2 x thick glass 8 - 10 - 12 mm	500 x 260	28,5 - 36,5	12	8,00
2 x reflecting glass 5 mm	300 x 270	22,5	12	6,00
2 x reflecting glass 6 mm	500 x 300	24,5	12	6,00
2 x reflecting glass 8 mm	500 x 300	28,5	12	9,00
2 x reflecting glass 10 + 12 mm	500 x 300	32,5 - 36,5	12	10,00

LZR (Spacer) The space between two sheets of glass.

Glass tiles, of various types and sizes

Type	size mm	Thickness mm
Primalit *square*	200 x 200	60
Primalit *rectangular*	270 x 150	60
Baldulux *square*	200 x 200	33,5
Baldulux *rectangular*	305 x 147	33,5
Great Baldulux *rectangular*	360 x 190	38,5
Gemax *square*	190 x 190	37,5
Catolux	300 x 60	40
Nevada *C - 32 y L - 32*	200 x 200	32

Characteristics of various types of rocks

Type	Hardness	Abrasivness	Shearability	Color
sandstone	medium	very abrasive	yes	pale tan
basalt	very hard	very abrasive	no	dark
limestone	variable	mildly abrasive	yes	pale
quartzite	very hard	very abrasive	no	variable
schist	hard	mildly abrasive	no	dark
granite	very hard	very abrasive	no	pale with dark grains
marble	very hard	mildly abrasive	no	various colors and veins
slate	hard	mildly abrasive	yes	dark bluish gray

Standard characteristics of rocks

Denomination	Resistance lb/inch^2	Density liq/inch^3	Structure	Applications
Sedimentary				
alabaster	568.8-1422	1.6	compact - crystal	carving and decor.
plaster of Paris	low	1.6	laminar - fibrous	plaster
sandstone	7110 - 25596	1.9 - 1.6	micro - grained	carving
build. limestone	medium	1.6	micro - grained	ashlar stone
kiln limestone	8532 - 28440	1.5 - 1.83	compact	various, quick lime
calcite	low	1.6 - 1.6	laminar	marble
conglomerate	8532 - 25596	1.33 - 2	macro - grained	fills
dolomitic	9954 - 14220	1.5 - 1.6	crystal like	carving
margarite	low	1.6	compact	quick lime
flint	high	1.6	compact	carving
Eruptive				
basalt	35550 - 42660	1.6 - 1.83	compact	various
diabase	17064 - 42660	1.6	compact	various
diorite	18486 - 32706	1.6	granitic	various
gabbro	21330 - 35550	1.6 - 1.83	grained	carving
granite	21330 - 38394	1.6 - 2	grained	many uses
ophite	21330 - 35550	1.83	crystal - granitic	ashlar, construction
olivine	36972 - 42660	2 - 2.17	grained	ashlar
porphyry	21330 - 36972	1.6 - 1.83	semi - granitic	carving, construction
serpentine	34128 - 35550	1.6	fibrous - leafy	carving, marbles
siennite	18486 - 32706	1.6	crystal - granitic	various
Metamorphic				
quartzite	7110 - 19908	1.6 - 1.6	compact	ashlar, paving
marble	8532 - 21330	1.6 - 1.83	compact	ornamental
gneiss	21330 - 39816	1.6	strato-crystalline	fill
slate	8532 - 12798	1.6 - 1.83	shearable	carving
Volcanic				
pumice	low		micro-grained	grindstone, fill

Characteristics of various types of rocks

Type	Hardness	Abrasivness	Shearability	Color
sandstone	medium	very abrasive	yes	pale tan
basalt	very hard	very abrasive	no	dark
limestone	variable	mildly abrasive	yes	pale
quartzite	very hard	very abrasive	no	variable
schist	hard	mildly abrasive	no	dark
granite	very hard	very abrasive	no	pale with dark grains
marble	very hard	mildly abrasive	no	various colors and veins
slate	hard	mildly abrasive	yes	dark bluish gray

Standard characteristics of rocks

Denomination	Resistance kg/cm^2	Density g/cm^3	Structure	Applications
Sedimentary				
alabaster	40 - 100	2,6	compact - crystal	carving and decor.
plaster of Paris	low	2,5	laminar - fibrous	plaster
sandstone	500 - 1800	1,9 - 2,6	micro - grained	carving
build. limestone	medium	2,6	micro - grained	ashlar stone
kiln limestone	600 - 2000	2,4 - 2,8	compact	various, quick lime
calcite	low	2,6 - 2,8	laminar	marble
conglomerate	600 - 1800	2,0 - 3,0	macro - grained	fills
dolomitic	700 - 1000	2,4 - 2,6	crystal like	carving
margarite	low	2,6	compact	quick lime
flint	high	2,6	compact	carving
Eruptive				
basalt	2500 - 3000	2,7 - 2,9	compact	various
diabase	1200 - 3000	2,6	compact	various
diorite	1300 - 2300	2,6	granitic	various
gabbro	1500 - 2500	2,5 - 2,8	grained	carving
granite	1500 - 2700	2,5 - 3,0	grained	many uses
ophite	1500 - 2500	2,8	crystal - granitic	ashlar, construction
olivine	2600 - 3000	3,0 - 3,4	grained	ashlar
porphyry	1500 - 2600	2,6 - 2,8	semi - granitic	carving, construction
serpentine	2400 - 2500	2,6	fibrous - leafy	carving, marbles
siennite	1300 - 2300	2,6	crystal - granitic	various
Metamorphic				
quartzite	500 - 1400	2,5 - 2,7	compact	ashlar, paving
marble	600 - 1500	2,5 - 2,8	compact	ornamental
gneiss	1500 - 2800	2,6	strato-crystalline	fill
slate	600 - 900	2,6 - 2,8	shearable	carving
Volcanic				
pumice	low		micro-grained	grindstone, fill

Denomination and applications of various plastics

Abreviation	Plastic	Uses
ABS	acryl-butadene-styrene	cold water tubing
EP	epoxy resin	veneers
EPS	expanded polystyrene	synthetic foam insulation
GF - UP	fiberglass polyester	facing, panels, cast items
MF	formaldehyde melamine	laminated plastics, adhesives
PA	polyamide (nylon)	wiring insulation, washers, clothing
PC	polycarbonate	secutity glazing
PE	polyethylene	electrical insulation, flooring, tubing
PF	phenolic formaldehyde (bakelite)	electrical insulation, accessories for doors
PMMA	polymethacrylate (acrylic glass, Perspex)	sanitary tiling, transparent sheets
PP	polypropylene	electrical insulation, tubing
PS	polystyrene	insulation, suspended ceilings
PU	polyurethane	insulation, paints
PVC	polyvinyl chloride	flooring materials and wall veneers
UP	unsaturated polyester resin	paints, asphalt sheeting

Insulation

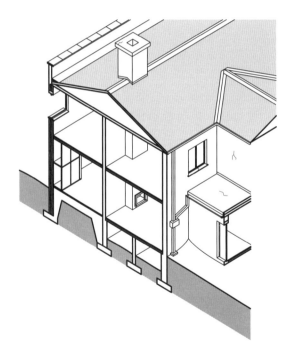

Characteristics of insulating materials

Fibrous insulating materials	Form, utilization	Temperature limit °C	Corrosion	Fire resistance	Mechanical resistance	Water absorb. resist.	Specific weight lb/ft³	Coefficient of conductivity W/m°K
Asbestos	flock, panels, flakes	500-600	No	very good	good in agglutinants	very poor	10-12.51 (160-200kg/m³)	0°C 0.04 50°C 0.042 100°C 0.047
Fiberglass	normal, refractory with resin	500-700	No, depends on type of resin	total, depending on type of resin	weak, depending on resin type	very poor	0.25-12.51 (4-200kg/m³)	0°C 0.039 50°C 0.041 100°C 0.046
Rock wool	flock, panels, flakes, fibers with an agglutinant.	600-700	Depends on type of resin and sulfite content	total except with resin	weak, depending on resin type	very poor	1.88-18.77 (30-300kg/m³)	0°C 0.04-0.042 50°C 0.042-0.048 100°C 0.047-0.057
Animal and vegetable fibers	flakes, anti-condensers	80	No	very poor	medium	very poor	12.51 (200 kg/m³)	0°C 50°C 100°C

Characteristics of insulating materials

Granular insulating materials	Form, utilization	Temperature limit °C	Corrosion	Fire resistance	Mechanical resistance	Water absorb. resist.	Specific weight lb/ft³	Coefficient of conductivity W/m°K
Perlite expanded volcanic material	in bulk, granules, panels, flakes	-200 - +900	No	good	weak	poor	2.5-6.26 (40-100kg/m³)	-50°C 0.04, 0°C 0.045, 50°C 0.052, 100°C 0.058
Vermiculite expanded aluminum and magnesium silicate	used for fire resistant concrete, flakes, panels	1000	No, only the agglutinant	very good, except the agglutinant.	weak, depending on agglutinant	very poor	4.38-6.88 (70-110kg/m³)	50°C 0.092, 100°C 0.095
Calcium silicate	panels, flakes	900	Attacks the aluminum, asphaltic protection	good	good	very poor	12.51 (200 kg/m³)	50°C 0.055, 100°C 0.062
Magnesium hydrated magnesium carbonate	panels, flakes in gross (weight or volume)	300	Attacks the aluminum, asphaltic protection	good	good	very poor	12.51 (200 kg/m³)	

Characteristics of insulating materials

Celular insulation	Form, utilization	Temperature limit °C	Corrosion	Fire resistance	Mechanical resistance	Resist. water absorb	Specific weight lb/ft³	Coefficient of conductivity W/mºK
Expanded cork	powder, granules, panels, flakes	-100 - +80	No	bad	good	poor	6.26-12.51 (100-200kg/m³)	-50°C 0.04 / 0°C 0.047 / 50°C 0.052
Glass foam	panels, flakes.	-200 - +450	No	very good	good	excel.	8.13-10.01 (130-160kg/m³)	-50°C 0.043 / 0°C 0.05 / 50°C 0.059 / 100°C 0.068
Expanded concrete	panels, flakes, bricks	-20 - +120	No	good	good	very poor	50.06-125.14 (800-2000 kg/m³)	0°C 0.071 / 50°C 0.079 / 100°C 0.085
Expanded synthetic resins *Urea formol Poliéster etc.*	For use at low temps.	-170 - +170 according to type	No	medium to poor	medium	varies with cell type	0.63-5 (10-80 kg/m³)	Usually from 0.029 to 0.035

Characteristics of insulating materials

Reflectant insulation	Form, utilization	Temperature limit °C	Corrosion	Fire reistance	Mechanical resistance	Water absorb. resist.	Specific weight lb/ft³	Coefficient of conductivity Kcal/hm°C
Thin metal sheets separated by a layer of air	aluminum sheets separated by a corrugated sheet	0 - 500	No	good	very poor	poor	0.19 (3kg/m³)	0.04 - 0.065
Super-insulat. (1)fibrous or expanded membranes. (2)reflectant membranes with micro-fibers.	Reflectant membranes enclosing a void within an airtight shell	-270 - +1000	No	total	depends on the shell	perfect	(1) 6.26-15.64 (100-250kg/m³) (2) 0.5-7.51 (8-120kg/m³)	(1) 0.1 of normal insulating materials (2) 0.1 of normal insulating materials

Typical causes of humidity in buildings

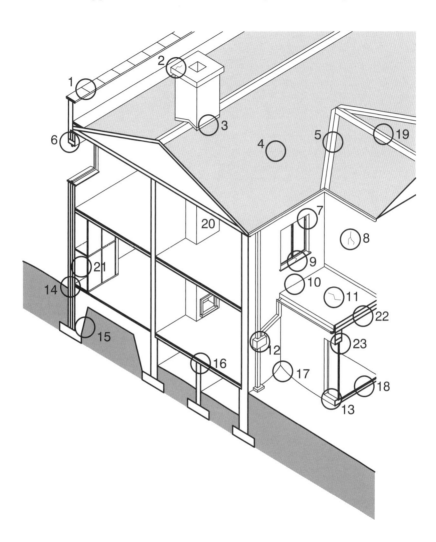

Penetration by water
1. No waterproofing beneath the coping tiles on the parapet
2. Faulty chimney hood
3. Faulty chimney flashing
4. Tiles, loose or broken
5. Faulty flashing of the roof valley
6. No weather strip above the window head
7. Faulty painting of the window frames
8. Cracks in the rendering of the walls
9. Cracks in the window sill
10. Asphaltic sheet on walls is insufficient
11. Cracks in the asphaltic insulation on a flat roof
12. Drainage, broken or blocked
13. No drip or weather molding to shed stormwater
14. Faulty plastering of the joints of a hollow wall

Rising damp
15. Uninsulated retaining walls
16. No insulation under the floor or over the foundation walls
17. The surrounding grade is higher than the waterproof layer
18. Faulty insulation under the floor

Condensation
19. Unventilated air space under the roof
20. No ventilating brick in the flue
21. Damp walls inside unventilated cupboards
22. Flat roofs with no vapour barrier
23. Condensation on the inside of a solid concrete lintel

Reduccion of noise transmitted through a building

Item	Reducción (dB)
9.5 mm plasterboard	25
Built-in cupboard	25 - 35
75 mm wooden wall, plastered on both sides	36
115 mm brick wall, plastered on both sides	47
230 mm brick wall, plastered on both sides	55
6 mm single pane of glass	29
6 mm double pane of glass with 100 mm air chamber	44
Door jamb without an impact damper	20
Door jamb with an impact damper	30
Heavy twin door with an impact damper	40
Unsealed single window sash	15
Well sealed single window sash	25

Design: basic principles of noise reduction

1. Orienting the building so that doors and windows do not face sources of noise.
2. Using sound barriers such as trees or other noise absorbing elements.
3. Separating noisy buildings from other quieter areas.
4. Keeping the sources of noise in a building as distant as possible.
5. Solid materials (concrete, bricks) offer the greatest acoustical protection.
6. Rugs and carpets greatly reduce impact noise.
7. Items that pierce walls (such as electrical connection boxes) may transmit a lot of noise. A 1 inch square hole through a plaster panel wall doubles the transmision of sound.
8. The transmision of sound through joints and holes can often be prevented the same way waterproofing is achieved. Noisy machinery should be avoided and shock absorbing materials should surround sources of vibration.

Building inspection and detecting flaws

Building inspection and detecting flaws

In the following tables we offer the most important flaws that a building is likely to present. They are ordered according to the parts of the building, starting with the support structures and the materials in each part. Each flaw is described together with its most probable causes. Thus the following diagrams can be used as a guideline to carry out the inspection of a buildng.

Item	Material	Flaw	Description	Possible causes
Foundations *retaining walls, footing, piles*	All	Settlement	Leaning, collapse, breakage	Soil failure, footing insufficiently wide, increased load
		Cracking	Vertical or horizontal cracking	Mechanical actions and deformations
	Brickwork or reinforced concrete	Physical erosion	Crumbling, loss of surface material	Absorption of water and freezing
		Chemical erosion	Patinas, alveolation, cement loss, crusting, efflorescences	Absorption of water and contamination
	Reinforced concrete	Cracking	Persistant localized cracking	Hygrothermal variations
			Localized cracking along the reinforcement members	Corrosion of the reinforcement
	Wood shoring, piles	Biological erosion	Galleries with body loss	xylophagous insects
			Bluish staining	Chromogenic fungi
			Rot, disintegration and body loss, with biological colonization	Rot provoking fungi

195

Item	Material	Flaw	Description	Possible causes
Load bearing walls	All	Settlement	Leaning, collapse, breakage	Soil failure, footing insufficiently wide, increased load
		Leaning	Loss of verticality	Settlement
		Warping	Loss of horizontality	Settlement, footing insufficiently wide, increased load
		Buckling	Loss of horizontality	Footing insufficiently wide, increased load
		Crack	Vertical cracking, persistent slanted cracking, Cracks in bearing arches.	Prior settlement
			Vertical cracks where support members meet floor	Soil movement caused by another member
			Vertical cracks or hollows	Thermal variation
		Fissure	Vertical or horizontal cracks	Mechanical actions and deformations
	Brickwork or reinforced concrete	Physical erosion	Crumbling, loss of surface material	Absorption of water and freezing
		Chemical erosion	Patinas, alveolation, crusts, decementation, efflorescences	Absorption of water and
	Reinforced concrete	Fissure	Local and persistent cracking	Hygrothermal variation
			Localized cracking following the line of internal reinforcement	Corrosion of reinforcement members
	Wood		The same as in foundations	

Item	Material	Flaw	Description	Possible causes
Pillars	All	leaning	Loss of verticality	Settlement
		Warping	Loss of horizontality	Settlement, footing insufficiently wide, increased load
		Buckling	Loss of horizontality	Footing insufficiently wide, increased load
		Fissure	Horizontal break due to buckling	Mechanical actions and deformations
	Brickwork or reinforced concrete	Physical erosion	Crumbling, loss of surface material	Water absorption and freezing
		Chemical erosion	Patinas, alveolation, crusting decementation, efflorescences	Water absorption and
	Reinforced concrete	Crack	Horizontal crack at the head	Soil pushed by another structural member. Thermal movement.
		Fissure	Persistent localized fissures	Hygrothermal movements
			Localized fissures following the internal reinforcement	Corrosion of reinforcement
	Wood	Biological erosion	Galleries with loss of material	Xylophagous insects
			Bluish staining	Chromogenic fungi
			Disintegration, with loss of material, biological colonization	Rot provoking fungi
	Metal	Corrosion	General loss of material	Oxidation prior to Immersion
			Localized loss of material	Unbalanced ventilation. Galvanic corrosion.

197

flaws of the structural members

Item	Material	Flaw	Description	Possible causes
Beams Waffle slabs Slabs	All	Warping	Loss of horizontality	Settlement, footing insufficiently wide, increased load
		Deflection	Loss of straightness	Footing insufficiently wide, increased load
		Fissure	Slanted fissure by deflection Horizontal fissures at the base by deflection	Mechanical actions and deformations
	Brickwork or reinforced concrete	Physical erosion	Crumbling, loss of surface material	Water absorption and freezing
	Chemical erosion	Patinas, alveolation, crusting decementation, efflorescences	Water absorption and
	Reinforced concrete	Crack	Vertical crack	Prior settlement Thermal movement
			Slanted crack at the support point	Soil pushed by another structural member.
		Fissure	Persistent localized fissures	Hygrothermal movements
			Localized fissures following the inner reinforcement	Corrosion of reinforcement members
	Wood	Biological erosion	Crevasses with loss of material	Xylophagous insects
			Coloración azulada	Chromogenic fungi
			Disintegration with loss of material biological colonization	Rot producing fungi
	Metal	Corrosion	General loss of material	Oxidation prior to immersion
			Localized loss of material	Unbalanced ventilation. Galvanic corrosion.

Item	Material	Flaw	Description	Possible causes
Arches Vaults Shells	All	Collapse	Deviation from a straight axis	Settlement, leaning, footing insufficiently wide, increased load.
		Cracks (in vaults)	Linear crack along a longitudinal axis.	Soil pushed by another structural member. Previous settlement.
			Crack perpendicular to the axis.	Previous settlement.
	Brickwork or reinforced concrete	Physical erosion	Crumbling, loss of surface material	Water absorption and freezing
	Chemical erosion		Patinas, alveolation, crusting, decementation, , eflorescences	Water absorption and contamination
	Reinforced concrete	Fissure	Localized and persistent fissures	Hygrothermal movements
			Localized fissures along the inner reinforcement members	Corrosion of reinforcement members
			Linear cracks along the curve of an arch	Mechanical actions and deformations.
	Wood	Biological erosion	Crevasses with loss of material	Xylophagous insects
			Bluish staining	Chromogenic fungi
			Disintegration, loss of material, biological colonization.	Rot provoking fungi
	Metal	Corrosion	General loss of material	Rusting due to immersion
			Localized loss of material	Unbalanced ventilation. Galvanic corrosion.

Item	Flaw	Description	Possible causes
Façade	Humidity near thermal bridges	Damp stains. Eflorescencies. Detachments. Erosion.	Interstitial condensation.
	Humidity at the bottom of an exterior wall or façade	Damp stains. Eflorescencies. Detachments. Erosion.	Ground water rising through the walls, absorbed by capilarity.
		Damp stains.	Hydroscopic condensation.
	Humidity of the interior finish of a façade	Damp stains. Drops of water. Fungi.	Superficial interior condensation.
	Cracks	Vertical.	Thermal actions.
		Horizontal cracks, at 45⁰ or in a load bearing arch.	Mechanical actions. (settlement, deflection, buckling, vertical loads, horizontal pressures.)
	Crevasses	Various types of crevasses.	Reaction to external forces.
		Various types of vertical and horizontal crevasses.	Thermal action.
		Various crevasses in the finish.	Faulty materials.
	Physical erosion	Meteorization.	Meteorological agents.
	Chemical erosion	Patinas. Crusts. Alveolation. Decementation.	Rain. Humidity. Contamination.
	Oxidation of metallic elements	Oxidation	Lack of protection.
	Corrosion of metallic elements	Loss of material.	Oxidation caused by immmersion. Unbalanced ventilation. Galvanic par. Intergranular corrosion.

Item	Flaw	Description	Possible causes
Partitions	Humidity	Damp stains. Eflorescencies. Detachments. Erosion.	Ground water rising through the walls, absorbed by capilarity.
		Damp stains.	Hydroscopic condensation.
	Crevasses	Verticales.	Thermal action.
		Horizontal cracks, at 45⁰ or in a load bearing arch.	Mechanical action. (settlement, deflection, buckling, vertical loads, horizontal pressures.)
	Cracks	Various types of crevasses.	As a reaction of the support.
		Various types of vertical and horizontal crevasses.	Thermal action.
		Various cracks in the finishes.	Faulty materials.
Reinforced concrete members	Cracks	Crevasses along the superficial reinforcement members.	Corrosion of the reinforcement.
Brickwork members	Humidity	Damp stains. Eflorescences. Blistering. Fungi	Application of the finish before reaching " equilibrium moisture".
	Organisms (arachnids)	Spider nests.	Hollows and cracks.
Wooden members	Organisms (xilophagi)	Destruction by galleries.	Humidity and lack of care (coleoptera) Insect colonies nearby (termites)
	Organisms (fungi)	Rot. Staining.	Humidity. Lack of ventilation.
Members made of porous materials	Organisms (fungi)	Stains.Smells. Biochemical erosion .	Humidity. Lack of ventilation and maintenance.
	Organisms (lichens and moss)	Stains.	Humidity. Lack of ventilation and maintenance.

Flaws of the walls, partitions and finishes

Item	Flaw	Description	Possible causes
Flooring, mopboard, dado	Mechanical erosion	Wear, detached crusts, scratches.	Impacts. Abrasion.
Rendering, parging and	Fissures	Network of cracks	Hydraulic shrinking.
	Dtetachments	Detachment and collapse of finish.	Surface stress due to expansion, contraction or elastic deformation. Internal expansion due to freezing or crystalization of mineral salts.
Roofing, eaves, cornices, windows, terraces	Damp	Damp stains. Efflorescencies. Detachment. Erosion.	Failure or absence of adequate waterproofing. Cracks or crevasses. Excessive porosity.
Stretches of wall above balconies or moldings	Damp	Damp stains. Efflorescencies. Detachment. Erosion.	Water or humidity rising by capilarity from a horizontal platform projecting outward from the façade.
Fences	Cracks	Vertical.	Thermal actions.
		Horizontal cracks, at 45^0 or in a load bearing arch	Mechanical actions. (settlement, deflection, buckling, vertical loads, horizontal pressures.)

Installations

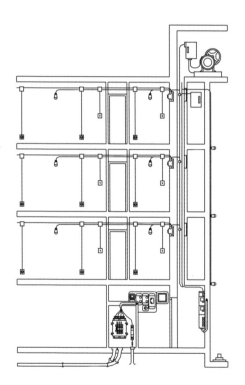

Heating systems by steam

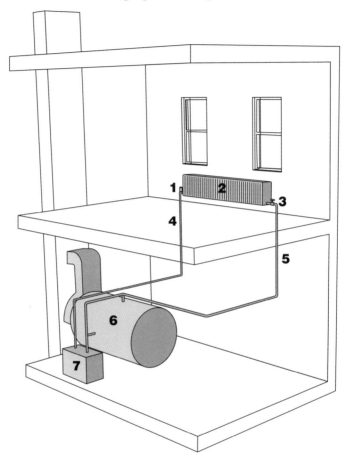

1 Steam lock
2 Convector radiator
3 Valve
4 Return pipe (water)
5 Steam pipe
6 Boiler
7 Vacuum pump

Heating systems by hot water

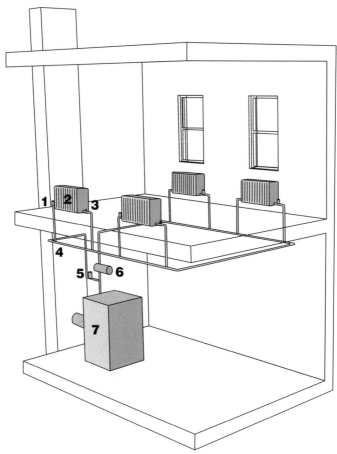

1   Air lock
2   Convector radiator
3   Control valve
4   Return system
5   Pump
6   Compression tank
7   Boiler

Heating systems by hot water

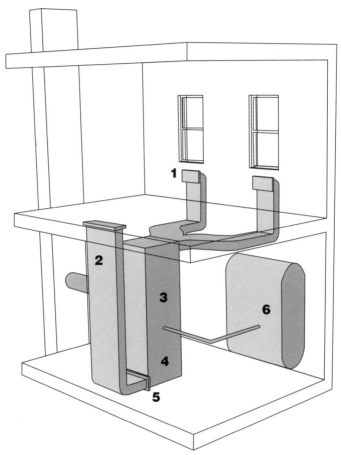

1 Supply tube
2 Return tube
3 Burner
4 fan
5 Dust filter
6 Fuel tank

Convector placement

| beneath a window | against a flat wall | freestanding (heating two spaces) | behind a bench |

 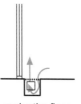

recessed in the wall   recessed in the wall   under the floor with an air suction device   under the floor with a cold air suction device

Radiator sizes

Panel radiators

Height: 11.81inch, 1ft 6 inch, 1ft 12 inch, 2 ft 4 inch *(300, 450, 600, 700 mm)*

Length: de 1 ft 4 inch (400mm) a 9 ft 10 inch (3000mm) cada 3.94 inch (100 mm)

Thickness: 1.85 inch (47 mm) (a panel without a convector)

       1.85 inch (47 mm) (a panel with a convector)

       3.03 inch (77 mm) (a double panel with a convector)

       3.94 inch (100 mm) (a double panel with a double convector)

Tube and fin radiators

Height: 7.28inch, 10.24inch, 11.81inch, 1ft 4inch, 1ft 6inch, 1ft 8inch, 1ft 10inch, 1ft 12inch, 2ft 6inch, 2ft 11inch, 3ft 3inch, 3ft 7inch, 3ft 11inch, 4ft 11inch, 5ft 11inch, 6ft 7inch, 7ft 3inch, 8ft 2inch, 9ft 2inch, 9ft 10inch, *(185, 260, 300, 400, 450, 500, 550, 600, 750, 900, 1000, 1100, 1200, 1500, 1800, 2000, 2200, 2500, 2800, 3000 mm)*

Thickness: 2.44inch *(62 mm)* (two fins), 3.94inch *(100 mm)* (three fins), 5.35inch *(136 mm)* (four fins), 6.81inch *(173 mm)* (five fins), 8.27inch *(210 mm)* (six fins).

Simple air conditioning system

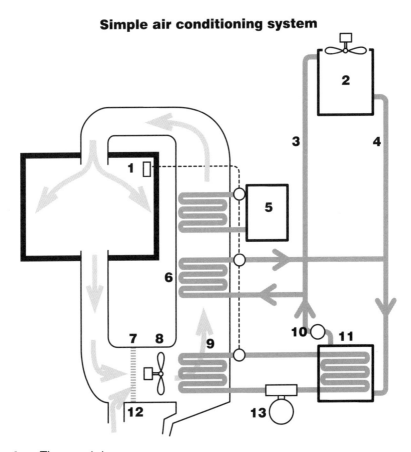

1   Thermostat
2   Refrigeration tower
3   Hot water
4   Cold water
5   Heating burner (winter)
6   Reheating coil (reduces moisture)
7   Filter
8   Fan
9   Hot side
10 Pump
11 Cold side
12 Outside air
13 Compressor

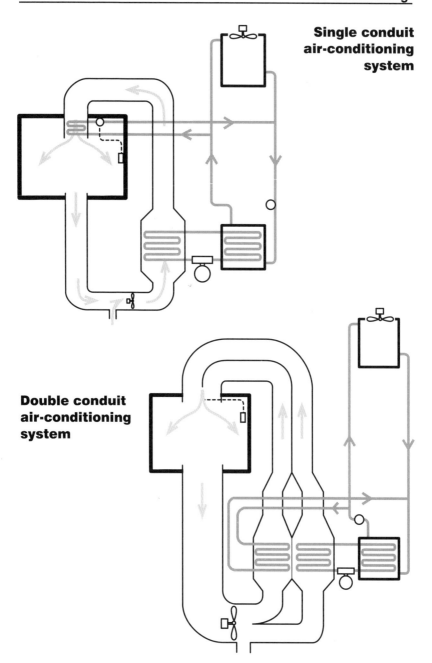

Single conduit air-conditioning system

Double conduit air-conditioning system

Characteristics of different types of lamps

	name	type	power
Incandescence	A	Universal standard use lamp	P (W) 60 - 200
	PAR 38	Parabolic reflector	P (W) 60 - 120
	PAR 56	Parabolic reflector	P (W) 300
	R	Reflector lamp	P (W) 60 - 150
	QT < 250	Incandescence lamp	P (W) 75 - 250
	QT > 250	Incandescence lamp	P (W) 300 - 1000
	QT - DE	Incandescence lamp	P (W) 200 - 500
Halogen lamps	QT - LV	Incandescence halogen lamp	P (W) 20 - 100
	QR - CB - LV	Incandescence halogen lamp	P (W) 20 - 75
	QR - 111 - LV	Incandescence halogen lamp	P (W) 35 - 100
Vapour lamps	HME	Mercury vapour lamp	P (W) 50 - 400
	HMR	Mercury vapour lamp	P (W) 80 - 125
	HST	Sodium vapour lamp	P (W) 35 - 100
	HSE	Sodium vapour lamp	P (W) 50 - 250
Metal salt halogen lamps	HIR	Metal halide reflector	P (W) 250
	HIT - DE	Metal halide lamp	P (W) 70 - 250
	HIT	Metal halide lamp	P (W) 35 - 150
	HIE	Metal halide lamp	P (W) 75 - 400
Fluorescent lamps	T	Fluorescent lamp	P (W) 18, 36, 58
	T	Compact fluorescent lamp	P (W) 7, 9, 11
	TC - D	Compact fluorescent lamp	P (W) 10, 13, 18, 26
	TC - L	Compact fluorescent lamp	P (W) 18, 24, 36
	TC - SB	Compact fluorescent lamp	P (W) 7, 11, 15, 20, 40, 55

Types of lamp for specific spaces

height of the space	nominal illumination intensity	type of space	A < 100	A > 100	PAR 38	PAR 56	R	QT < 250	QT > 250	QT-DE	QT-LV	QR-CB-LV	QR-LV	T	TC	TC-D	TC-L	HME < 80	HME > 80	HSE	HST	HIT-DE <70	HIT-DE >70	HIT <70	HIT >70	HIE
up to 9ft 10inch (3m)	up to 200 lx	Workshop												●												
		Restaurant	●					●		●	●	●														
		Lobby	●	●	●					●	●				●	●										
	up to 500 lx	Office													●	●	●									
		Meeting hall	●	●						●	●				●	●	●	●								
		Workshop													●				●	●						
		Bookshop							●						●		●									
		Shop							●	●					●	●	●	●					●		●	
		Exhibition space			●										●	●	●	●	●				●		●	
		Museum or art gallery	●	●	●	●	●	●	●	●					●	●	●	●	●							
		Entrance hall	●	●				●		●					●	●	●	●								
	up to 750 lx	Office													●		●									
		Workshop													●				●				●		●	
		Department store													●		●	●								
		Supermarket													●											
		Show window						●	●	●	●	●	●										●	●	●	●
		Hotel kitchen													●		●									
		Concert hall stage							●		●		●													
from 9ft 10inch (3m) to 16ft 5inch (5m)	up to 200 lx	Store													●				●	●	●	●				
		Workshop													●				●							
		Lobby	●	●	●					●					●	●										
		Restaurant	●						●	●	●	●			●	●										
		Church	●	●	●				●							●										
		Concert hall, theater	●	●					●																	
	up to 500 lx	Workshop													●				●				●		●	
		shop	●						●						●		●									
		Exhibition space							●						●	●	●	●					●		●	
		Entrance hall			●	●	●	●	●	●	●				●		●	●								
		Hotel	●	●					●						●	●	●	●					●		●	
	up to 750 lx	Workshop														●	●									
		Bookshop													●				●	●			●		●	●
		Exhibition space							●						●		●									
		Trade showroom													●		●	●					●		●	●
		Department store																	●							●
		Supermarket													●		●						●		●	●
		Industrial kitchen													●											
		Concert stage													●											
		Church				●	●		●	●																
more than 16ft 5inch (5m)	up to 200 lx	Concert hall						●	●	●																
		Museum						●	●	●																
	up to 500 lx	Airport and station							●	●								●		●						
		Convention hall													●			●		●	●	●		●		●	●
		Auditorium						●	●																	
	up to 750 lx	Exhibition space							●						●		●									
		Trade showroom											●		●		●							●	●	●
		Supermarket																	●					●	●	●
															●				●					●	●	●

Typical electrical installation for a building

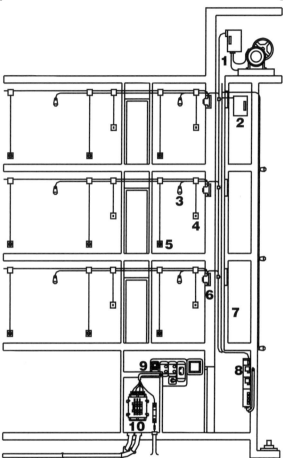

1 Mechanical power supply line
2 Antenna signal amplifier and distribution, and general power supply
3 Neutral
4 Phase
5 Protection
6 Main distribution box
7 Individual branch lines
8 Central meter box
9 Distribution line
10 General main fuse and protection box

Typical electrical installation for an apartment

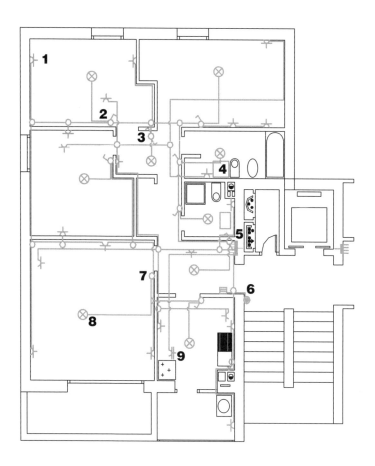

1   Single socket
2   Switch
3   Commuter switch
4   Washing machine
5   Distribution box
6   Door bell
7   Connection box
8   Light
9   Double socket

Water supply for an apartment building

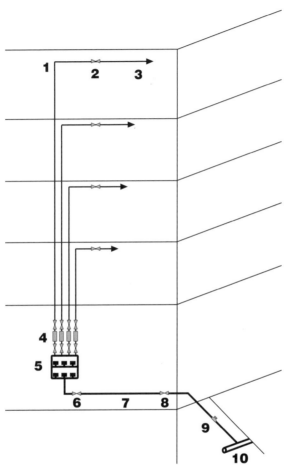

1 Riser
2 Private apartment shut off valve
3 Private distribution pipes in an apartment
4 Water meter with entrance and exit valves
5 Water meter box, containig the building's water meters
6 One way valve
7 Water supply branch
8 Main shut off valve of the building
9 Curb cock
10 Water main

Soil stack for a small building

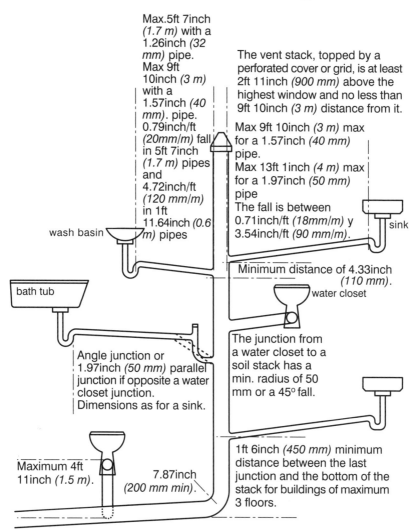

Max.5ft 7inch *(1.7 m)* with a 1.26inch *(32 mm)* pipe. Max 9ft 10inch *(3 m)* with a 1.57inch *(40 mm)*. pipe. 0.79inch/ft *(20mm/m)* fall in 5ft 7inch *(1.7 m)* pipes and 4.72inch/ft *(120 mm/m)* in 1ft 11.64inch *(0.6 m)* pipes

The vent stack, topped by a perforated cover or grid, is at least 2ft 11inch *(900 mm)* above the highest window and no less than 9ft 10inch *(3 m)* distance from it.

Max 9ft 10inch *(3 m)* max for a 1.57inch *(40 mm)* pipe. Max 13ft 1inch *(4 m)* max for a 1.97inch *(50 mm)* pipe The fall is between 0.71inch/ft *(18mm/m)* y 3.54inch/ft *(90 mm/m)*.

wash basin

sink

bath tub

Minimum distance of 4.33inch *(110 mm)*. water closet

Angle junction or 1.97inch *(50 mm)* parallel junction if opposite a water closet junction. Dimensions as for a sink.

The junction from a water closet to a soil stack has a min. radius of 50 mm or a 45° fall.

Maximum 4ft 11inch *(1.5 m)*.

7.87inch *(200 mm min)*.

1ft 6inch *(450 mm)* minimum distance between the last junction and the bottom of the stack for buildings of maximum 3 floors.

Dimensions of open fireplaces

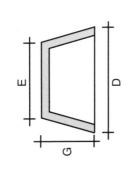

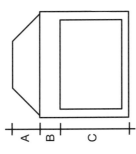

	Open on one side					Open on two sides			Open on three sides		
Floor surface of the room.	0-16	16-22	22-30	30-35	33-40	25-35	35-45	48-	35-45	45-55	55-
Size of the fireplace opening.	60/46	70/52	80/58	90/64	100/71						
Diameter of flue.	20	22	25	30	30						
Dimensions: A	22.5	24	25.5	28	30	25	30	35	25	30	35
B	13.5	15	15	21	21	30	30	30	30	30	30
C	52	58	64	71	78	50	58	65	50	58	65
D	72	84	94	105	115	77	90	108	77	90	114
E	50	60	65	75	93	77	90	108	77	90	114
F	19.5	19.5	22.5	26	26	27.5	30	32.5	27.5	30	32.5
G	42	47	51	55	59	64	71	82	64	71	82

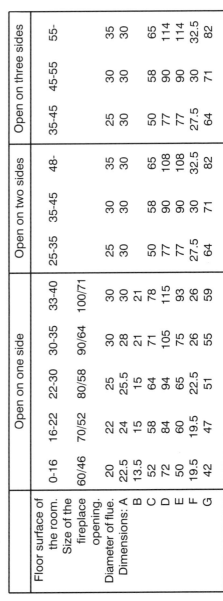

	Open on one side (inch)					Open on two sides (inch)			Open on three sides (inch)		
Floor surface of the room.	0-6.24	6.24-8.58	8.58-11.7	11.7-13.65	12.87-15.6	9.75-13.65	13.65-17.55	18.72-	13.65-17.55	17.55-21.45	21.45-
Size of the fireplace opening.	23.4/17.94	27.3/20.28	31.2/22.62	35.1/24.96	39/27.69						
Diameter of flue.	7.8	8.58	9.75	11.7	11.7	9.75	11.7	13.65	9.75	11.7	13.65
Dimensions: A	8.78	9.36	9.95	10.92	11.7	11.7	11.7	11.7	11.7	11.7	11.7
B	5.27	5.85	5.85	8.19	8.19						
C	20.28	22.62	24.96	27.69	30.42	19.5	22.62	25.35	19.5	22.62	25.35
D	28.08	32.76	36.66	40.95	44.85	30.03	35.1	42.12	30.03	35.1	44.46
E	19.5	23.4	25.35	29.25	36.27	30.03	35.1	42.12	30.03	35.1	44.46
F	7.61	7.61	8.78	10.14	10.14	10.73	11.7	12.68	10.73	11.7	12.68
G	16.38	18.33	19.89	21.45	23.01	24.96	27.69	31.98	24.96	27.69	31.98

Unit conversion tables

length conversion factors

CUSTOMARY	METRIC I.S.
1 mile	1,609344 km
1 chain	20,1168 m
1 yard	0,9144 m
1 foot	0,3048 m
1 inch	25,4 mm

METRIC I.S.	CUSTOMARY
1 kilometer	0,621371 miles 49,7096 chains
1 meter	3,28084 feet 1,09361 yards
1 milimeter	0,039370 inch
1 micrometer	0,0003937 inch

Surface area conversion factors

CUSTOMARY	METRIC I.S.
1 mile^2	2,59000 km^2
1 acre	4046,87m^2 0,404687 ha
1 yard^2	0,836127 m^2
1 foot^2	0,092903 m^2
1 inch^2	645,16 m^2

METRIC I.S.	CUSTOMARY
1 km^2	0,386101 miles^2
1 ha	2,47104 acres
1 m^2	10,7639 foot^2 1,9599 yard^2
1 mm^2	0,001550 inch^2

Volume conversion factors

CUSTOMARY	METRIC I.S.
1 acre foot	1233,49 m^3
1 yard^3	0,764555 m^3
1 foot^3	28316,8 cm^3
1 inch^3	16,3871 cm^3

METRIC I.S.	CUSTOMARY
1 m^3	acre ft 0,810709 x 10^3 1,30795 yard^3 423,776 board ftc 35,3147 ft^3
1 mm^3	cubic inch 61,0237 x 10^{-6}

Length conversions graphic scale

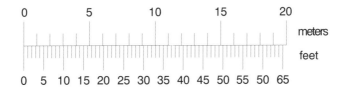

Temperature conversion factors

CUSTOMARY	METRIC I.S.
1°F	0,555556 °C
	5/9 °C o 5/9 K

METRIC I.S.	CUSTOMARY
1°C	1 K
	1/8 °F

Mass conversion factors

CUSTOMARY	METRIC I.S.
1 ton (short)	0,907 ton. metr.
	907,185 kg
1 lb (pound)	0,453592 Kg
1 oz (ounce	28,34959 g
1 pennyweight	1,55517 g

METRIC I.S.	CUSTOMARY
1 ton	2204,62 lb
1 kg	2,20462 lb
	35,274002 oz
1 g	0,35274 oz (ounce)
	0,643015 penny weight

Volume conversión factors

CUSTOMARY	METRIC I.S.
1 gal	3,78541 l
1 qt	946,353 ml
1 pt	473,177 ml
1 floz	29,5735 ml

METRIC I.S.	CUSTOMARY
1 L	0,03531477 ft ^{3}
	0,264172 gal
	1,05669 qt
1 mL	0,061023 in^3

temperature conversion graphic scale

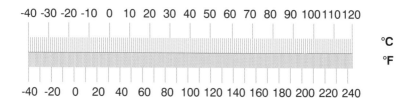

-40 -30 -20 -10 0 10 20 30 40 50 60 70 80 90 100 110 120   °C

°F

-40 -20 0 20 40 60 80 100 120 140 160 180 200 220 240

7 Kg are equal to 15,43 pounds

S.I.	1	2	3	4	5	6	7	8	9	10	CUSTOMARY
cm	0.39	0.79	1.18	1.57	1.97	2.36	2.76	3.15	3.54	3.94	inches
m	3.28	6.56	9.84	13.12	16.40	19.69	22.97	26.25	29.53	32.80	feet
m	1.09	2.19	3.28	4.37	5.47	6.56	7.66	8.75	9.84	10.94	yards
km	0.62	1.24	1.86	2.49	3.11	3.73	4.35	4.98	5.59	6.21	miles
cm^2	0.16	0.31	0.47	0.62	0.78	0.93	1.09	1.24	1.40	1.55	inches^2
m^2	1.20	2.39	3.58	4.78	5.98	7.18	8.37	8.37	9.57	10.76	feet^2
m^2	10.76	21.53	32.29	43.06	53.82	64.58	75.35	86.11	96.88	107.64	yards^2
ha	2.47	4.94	7.41	9.88	12.36	14.83	17.30	19.77	22.24	24.71	acre
cm^3	0.06	0.12	0.18	0.24	0.31	0.37	0.43	0.49	0.55	0.61	inches^3
m^3	35.31	70.63	105.94	141.26	176.57	211.89	247.20	282.52	317.83	353.85	feet^3
litros	0.04	0.07	0.11	0.14	0.18	0.21	0.25	0.28	0.32	0.35	feet^3
litros	0.22	0.44	0.66	0.88	1.10	1.32	1.54	1.76	1.98	2.20	GB gal
litros	0.26	0.53	0.79	1.06	1.32	1.59	1.85	2.11	2.38	2.64	USA gal
kg	2.21	4.41	6.61	8.82	11.02	13.23	15.43	17.67	19.84	22.05	pounds
kg/cm^2	14.22	28.45	42.67	56.90	71.12	85.34	99.56	113.79	128.01	142.23	lb/in^2
kN/m^2	0.145	0.290	0.435	0.580	0.725	0.870	1.015	1.160	1.305	1.450	lb/in^2
kg/m^3	0.062	0.125	0.187	0.250	0.312	0.375	0.437	0.499	0.562	0.624	lb/feet^3
m/s	2.24	4.47	6.71	8.95	11.18	13.42	15.66	17.90	20.13	22.37	miles/h

4 acres are equal to 1.62 **I.S.** hectares (ha,)

CUSTOMARY	1	2	3	4	5	6	7	8	9	10	I.S.
inches	2.54	5.08	7.62	10.16	12.70	15.24	17.78	20.32	22.86	25.40	cm
feet	0.31	0.61	0.91	1.22	1.52	1.83	2.13	2.44	2.74	3.05	m
yards	0.91	1.83	2.74	3.65	4.57	5.49	6.40	7.32	8.23	9.14	m
miles	1.61	3.22	4.83	6.44	8.05	9.66	11.27	12.87	14.48	16.09	km
inches^2	6.45	12.90	19.36	25.81	32.26	38.71	45.16	51.61	58.06	64.52	cm^2
feet^2	0.09	0.19	0.28	0.37	0.46	0.56	0.65	0.74	0.84	0.93	m^2
yardas^2	0.84	1.67	2.51	3.34	4.18	5.02	5.85	6.69	7.53	8.36	m^2
acre	0.40	0.81	1.21	1.62	2.02	2.42	2.83	3.23	3.64	4.05	ha
inches^3	16.39	32.77	49.16	65.55	81.94	98.32	114.71	131.10	147.48	163.87	cm^3
feet^3	0.03	0.06	0.08	0.11	0.14	0.17	0.20	0.23	0.25	0.28	m^3
feet^3	28.32	56.63	84.95	113.26	141.58	169.90	198.21	226.53	254.84	283.16	litros
Brit gal	4.55	9.09	13.64	18.18	22.73	27.28	31.82	36.37	40.91	45.46	litros
USA gal	3.79	7.57	11.36	15.14	18.93	22.71	26.50	30.28	34.07	37.85	litros
pounds	0.45	0.91	1.36	1.81	2.27	2.72	3.18	3.63	4.08	4.54	kg
lb/in^2	0.07	0.14	0.21	0.28	0.35	0.42	0.49	0.56	0.63	0.70	kg/cm^2
lb/in^2	6.9	13.79	20.68	27.58	34.48	41.37	48.26	55.16	62.06	68.95	kN/m^2
lb/feet^3	16.02	32.04	48.06	64.07	80.09	96.11	112.13	128.15	144.17	160.19	kg/m^3
miles/h	0.45	0.89	1.34	1.79	2.24	2.68	3.13	3.58	4.02	4.47	m/s